Grady McWhiney
The Civil War
A Concise Account by a Noted Southern Historian

Grady McWhiney
The Civil War

A Concise Account by a Noted Southern Historian

McWhiney Foundation Press
McMurry University
Abilene, Texas

Library of Congress Cataloging-in-Publication Data

McWhiney, Grady.
  The Civil War: a concise account by a noted Southern
  historian/Grady McWhiney; [foreword by John C. Waugh;
  introduction by Donald S. Frazier].—1st ed.
    p. cm.
  Includes bibliographical references.
  ISBN-13: 978-1-893114-49-4 (pbk.: alk. paper)
  ISBN-10: 1-893114-49-X (pbk.: alk. paper)
  1. United States—History—Civil War, 1861-1865. I. Title.
  E468.M32 2005
  973.7—dc22
                                                    2005027130

McWhiney Foundation Press
McMurry Station, Box 637
Abilene, TX 79697-0637
(325) 572-3974
(325) 572-3991 fax
www.mcwhiney.org/press

Printed in the United States of America

Distributed by Texas A&M University Press Consortium
www.tamu.edu/upress
1-800-826-8911

ISBN-13: 978-1-893114-49-4
ISBN-10: 1-893114-49-X
10 9 8 7 6 5 4 3 2

Book designed by Rosenbohm Graphic Design

Contents

Maps

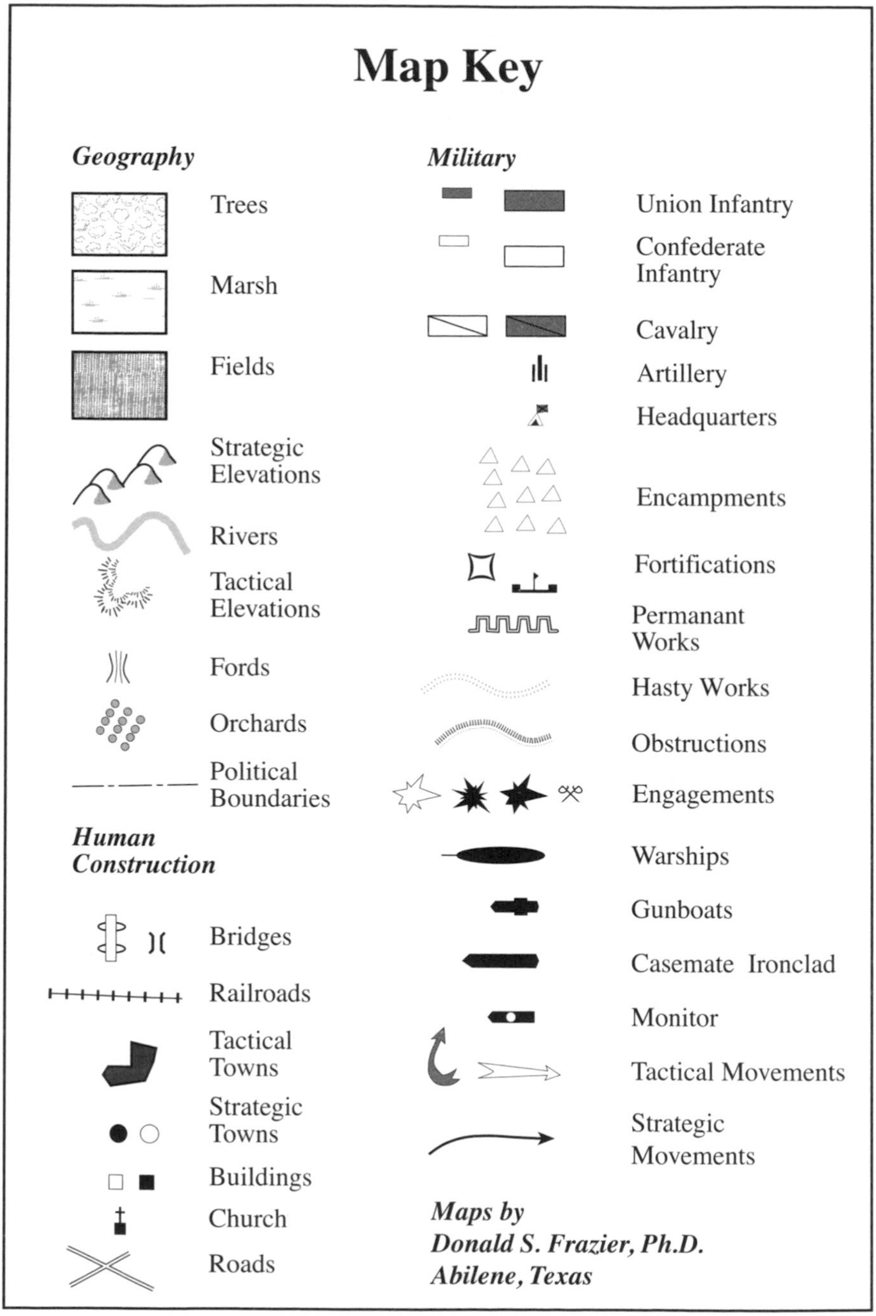

Map Key

Geography

Trees

Marsh

Fields

Strategic Elevations

Rivers

Tactical Elevations

Fords

Orchards

Political Boundaries

Human Construction

Bridges

Railroads

Tactical Towns

Strategic Towns

Buildings

Church

Roads

Military

Union Infantry

Confederate Infantry

Cavalry

Artillery

Headquarters

Encampments

Fortifications

Permanant Works

Hasty Works

Obstructions

Engagements

Warships

Gunboats

Casemate Ironclad

Monitor

Tactical Movements

Strategic Movements

Maps by
Donald S. Frazier, Ph.D.
Abilene, Texas

Foreword

The Civil War has been a twice-fought affair—the war itself lasting four years, and the writing about the war, which is likely to never end. The war itself showcased a host of generals, the best of them immortalized by their deeds. Repeatedly reincarnated in the 140 years since, the war has produced a host of historian-generals, the best of them immortalized by their research and their writings.

Among the very elite of this cadre of historian-generals is Grady McWhiney. For the better part of half a century he has stood in their foremost ranks. Preeminent among Southern historians specializing in the military history of the war, he has won repeated honors and admiration. As a teacher and mentor of other historians he also stands preeminent. His doctoral students scattered around the country are among the new generation of leading historians in this ongoing campaign to understand and interpret the Civil War.

But it is his skill in illuminating deep research with stylish writing that has elevated McWhiney into the front ranks of the historian-generals. This brief primer on the Civil War, telling its story from its roots through its bloody course to its end, showcases this talent to great effect.

It is not easy to condense that monumental struggle to a short concise narrative that is comprehensive, but still sings—to make it more than just a summary of dates and events. McWhiney has done far more than that. He has hit all the right buttons and done it with style, stitching an array of facts and events and perspective onto a fully wrought canvas brimming with quotes and meaning. To brevity he has added life, deftly describing the actors on that great stage, bringing them back alive, cogently and vividly.

There is very little to criticize in this work. I ask myself if I could do as well. Certainly I couldn't. His little book, uniting such a thorough knowledge of the war with a deft writing style is difficult to match. There are points you might argue. For instance he says President Abraham Lincoln could never get along with Gen. George B. McClellan. Rather, it seems to me, it was McClellan who couldn't get along with Lincoln. But this is needless nitpicking.

This little jewel on the Civil War begins where it should, logically, even-handedly, where the Union began showing sure signs of fraying—in the debates over the Missouri Compromise in 1820, through the Compromise of 1850, to the unraveling of all compromise following the passage of the Kansas-Nebraska Act of 1854. From these stage-setting events leading to disunion McWhiney takes us on through the war to its end, missing no vital link. You know that much has by necessity been left out, but you get the sense that everything that should be in a brief treatment of the war such as this is solidly there and that it is a very worthy and successful effort.

John C. Waugh
Author of *20 Good Reasons to Study the Civil War*

Introduction

From New Hampshire to Georgia, there were no united states in 1787. Instead, the colonial legacy of Great Britain had engendered a host of suspicions among thirteen former colonies, each with its own particular relationship to the other. Having been founded and raised as competitors, there was little of the cooperative spirit about them as the new nation, dubiously called these "United States," languished under a confederation form of government that had proven untenable. The singular form of the country's title that would carry it into the future, *The United States,* awaited a national reckoning.

Not only was the country politically divided in 1787, but its people harbored cultural animosities toward each other as well. To observers at the time, it was a "nation of nations." Regional, cultural, and a host of other biases tinctured the souls of most Americans and defined the version of the nation to whom they owed allegiance, a sort of kaleidoscope of definitions that undermined national consensus.

In the North, Puritan ancestry deeply colored New England. With their blood came a Calvinist burden as well. Intent on reforming human society and bettering their world, their sense of moral and intellectual superiority observed no borders. Wealth, and the industriousness that created it, were divine gifts. Honor came to those whose worldly successes marked them as blessed. Idleness was simply laziness.

In the southern tidewater, landed gentry had also emerged, descended in birth and deed from the English Cavaliers. These citizens considered such northern pursuits as unbefitting a person of gentle birth, but worthy of delegation to subordinates. Wealth was merely the means to such ends. Leisure, with its myriad enjoyments, was a noble goal. Honor among the Cavaliers came as birthright and as an heirloom to be defended and passed intact to future generations.

Beyond the fences of the Cavalier estates, there existed the sweepings of the "Celtic Fringe" of Great Britain. Composed of Scots, "mere" Irish, Scotch-Irish, and Borderers among others, these marginalized people had been both willing and unwilling immigrants to North America. Drawn to the wild places that resembled the old country, these "crackers," as they became known, became the quintessential frontiersmen of America. Work, so highly prized by their northern compatriots, seemed an intrusion into the sensual pursuits of life. Suspicious of authority and jealous of each other, these denizens of forest and mountain earned their honor by being prepared to die in its defense.

A host of hopeful, eager and anxious people from a score of African nations added to this mix. They had not come as immigrants to this new country, but rather as commodities imported in response to commercial demands. Yet, despite the efforts of many to ignore, marginalize, and cloak them, they remained— about one in five of the national population. Theirs was a perverse nationhood not of their own making or claim, but of shared calumny and calamity. This voiceless humanity would soon become the shadow cast by the bright light of liberty then dawning in America.

This disparate population had tried to live together in harmony since the earliest stirrings of revolution in 1775. They had united long enough to win, with the support of France, their independence in 1783. Without a common enemy, bickering resumed and the infant confederation of states failed. With the government deadlocked, the citizenry at odds, and the binding of the states becoming untied, the leaders of the revolution called a convention to be held in Philadelphia in 1787. What emerged was a new pattern for government, embodied in a written constitution.

The preamble of the U.S. Constitution, "We, the People, of the United States, in order to form a more perfect Union," promised much. For some, it held the promise of a form of government that would settle squabbles between sovereign states and bind them together in common cause. At the same time, this 1787 document seemed to bestow sovereignty upon individual citizens of the nation. That this document was meant as a permanent correction to a vexing issue facing the new nation, none would contest. The Constitution was a compact, a binding contract, and all parties viewed it as a victory. All parties also knew that many important issues had been deferred as well, in favor of national amity.

The new Constitution protected much. A collection of autonomous states emerging from the near anarchy of a confederation government guarded their rights and jurisdictions jealously. Even so, powers enumerated to the new government stopped well short of the taint of tyranny that many opponents had suggested. It appeared to be a perfection of the confederation already in place.

Much, though, remained subject to interpretation. Strict readers of the document were glad to see the powers of the government so clearly defined. So-called "elastic clauses" encouraged loose interpretations of the Constitution by implying that the various branches of government could behave in new and unforeseen ways as future circumstances required. Many fretted over this seemingly open-ended view, leading to the addition of a Bill of Rights. These ten amendments were supposed to restate, clearly, what were firmly held liberties under the new system. According to James Madison, instead of protecting civil liberties, these ten amendments merely opened the door to the spread, or usurpation, of power by an unchecked government. Simply stated, why list rights that cannot be violated, when a conservative reading of the document made it clear that the power to abridge these rights is not an enumerated power of the government anyway?

Much was at stake. Opponents of the Constitution feared that the confederation would be replaced by a stronger, more sinister federation where power no longer streamed from the people, but from the government. Instead of a bottom up system, as they hoped, loose interpreters would create a leviathan state where the government would instead dictate policies to the people. But, this remained a fear, and not a stated reality. Even with these tugs and challenges, the various states ratified the Constitution of the United States and embarked upon a new experiment.

When the framers of the document recessed from their 1787 meeting in Philadelphia, a crowd of townspeople awaited word on what the secret proceedings had been about. One shouted to Benjamin Franklin, president of the Constitutional convention, "what have you made?" "A Republic," he replied, "if we can keep it."

Almost immediately upon being adopted by the new nation in a very contentious process, competing factions emerged with visions of what the new nation should become. One faction, rallying behind the leadership of New Yorker Alexander Hamilton, viewed the future of the nation as an urban, industrial place. They held England as the example to emulate. Their opponents supported a rural, agricultural nation, the vision of Virginian Thomas Jefferson and, after 1789, they pointed to bucolic and republican France as a worthy model.

Essentially a nation of small farmers, the United States had geographic peculiarities that would dictate which man's vision would hold final sway. In the North, rugged hills and mountains rose near the sea. Northern streams ran fast, and the land yielded rocks as readily as a harvest. Mill wheels slapped these northern waters as the engines of industry encouraged a commercial class bent on production and trade. In the South, the mountains were hundreds of miles inland, and the waters there were dark, sluggish, and deep. Along their banks, the alluvial soil seemed eager to yield its bounty and only the access to labor limited a farmer's potential.

As a result, in the years after 1787, Americans would pursue, experiment with, and implement both the Hamiltonian and Jeffersonian views. The North, with its growing emphasis on manufacturing and commerce, served as an incubator for the Hamiltonian vision. The agrarian South, at first blush, seemed a Jeffersonian paradise.

The Constitution, that amazing document in which all factions believed that their view had held sway, left much unaddressed. Sectionalism, inherent in a nation composed of thirteen arguably sovereign states, had coalesced in two directions. Most of the framers had focused on expansion to the West and the status of newly added states. Under the Constitution, differences between the North and South went unresolved.

Both sides compromised on the issue of slavery in a political trade in exchange for southern support for ratification. Northerners could increasingly live without the institution since immigration and mechanization met the labor needs of their economy. In contrast, the South would remain a howling wilderness without a vast supply of labor to work its rich soils, and northern ship owners and capitalists were happy to supply. Most believed that slavery was doomed, soon to be overtaken by a rushing tide of progress, and politicians did forbid the importation of slaves in 1808. As a result, the slave trade slowly withered while slavery

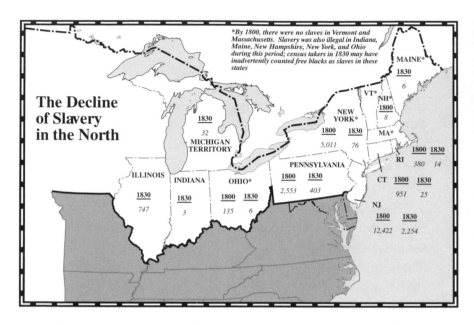

The Decline of Slavery in the North

By 1800, there were no slaves in Vermont and Massachusetts. Slavery was also illegal in Indiana, Maine, New Hampshire, New York, and Ohio during this period; census takers in 1830 may have inadvertently counted free blacks as slaves in these states

MAINE*
1830
6

MICHIGAN TERRITORY
1830
32

VT*
NH*
1800
8

NEW YORK*
1800 — 5,011
1830 — 76

MA*
RI
1800 — 380
1830 — 14

ILLINOIS
1830
747

INDIANA
1830
3

OHIO*
1800 — 135
1830 — 6

PENNSYLVANIA
1800 — 2,553
1830 — 403

CT
1800 — 951
1830 — 25

NJ
1800 — 12,422
1830 — 2,254

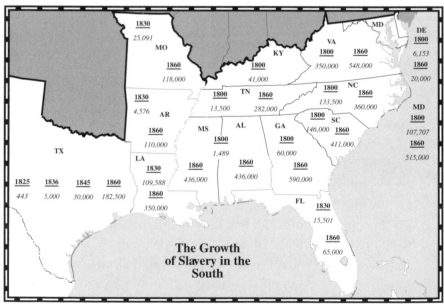

The Growth of Slavery in the South

MO
1830 — 25,091
1860 — 118,000

KY
1800 — 41,000
1860 — ...

VA
1800 — 350,000
1860 — 548,000

MD
DE
1800 — 6,153
1860 — 20,000

AR
1830 — 4,576
1860 — 110,000

TN
1800 — 13,500
1860 — 282,000

NC
1800 — 133,500
1860 — 360,000

MD
1800 — 107,707
1860 — 515,000

MS
1800 — 1,489
1860 — 436,000

AL
1800 — ...
1860 — 436,000

GA
1800 — 60,000
1860 — 590,000

SC
1800 — 146,000
1860 — 411,000

TX
1825 — 443
1836 — 5,000
1845 — 30,000
1860 — 182,500

LA
1830 — 109,588
1860 — 350,000

FL
1830 — 15,501
1860 — 65,000

itself became protected by the Constitution, its chattel counting as 3/5th a human being for purposes of representation.

Even so, the South's "peculiar institution" seemed limited in scope. First introduced in Virginia in 1619, African slaves had promised much, including resistance to warm climate diseases, familiarity with agriculture, and great stamina. Their race, too, kept them identifiable as a class even though many were later granted their freedom along the same pattern as white indentures. As planters made more money in cash crops such as tobacco, rice, and indigo, slaves became too valuable to lose after a length of service, and their status became permanent.

The nature of these cash crops, though, limited the spread of slavery outside of a particular region. In the case of tobacco, production techniques did not require great numbers of slaves for the farm to be profitable. Accountants argued as well as to the profitability of slavery, since the care and feeding of the bondspeople consumed up to 2/3rds of what income they produced. One crop, cotton, seemed to hold great promise but refining techniques limited its viability. It was easy to grow, was in increasing demand among world textile mills, and even farmers of modest means could afford to cultivate the crop. Removing the seeds from the lint was a time-consuming and, in terms of man-hours, expensive proposition. In short, planters could easily grow and sell more cotton than they could refine.

A Connecticut schoolteacher named Eli Whitney with a genius for invention inadvertently breathed life back into the institution. Having been hired as a tutor on a Georgia plantation in 1793, Whitney tinkered with a device that deseeded cotton. This "cotton engine" or "gin," reversed the equation, allowing as much cotton as was grown to be refined for commercial use.

This simple device would open the once exclusive world of the landed planter to middle class entrepreneurs. With a small

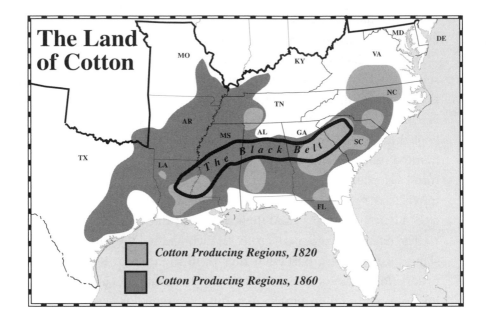

The Land of Cotton

MD
DE
MO
KY
VA
NC
TN
AR
MS
AL
GA
SC
TX
LA
The Black Belt
FL

☐ *Cotton Producing Regions, 1820*

☐ *Cotton Producing Regions, 1860*

amount of money, an average farmer could purchase acreage previously considered ill suited for cash crops. With the aid of a small number of slaves, he could work the land, harvest enough cotton to pay his creditors, and own his farm outright in a short time. From there, he could expand his operation, limited only by the amount of land and the number of slaves available. This reality fueled a new demand for both commodities.

The great prize, then, was the West. More lands, abundant resources, and the liberty of the frontier meant that enterprising men could make their fortunes. The scions of bold men could then, by moving further toward the setting sun, have a fortune as large or larger than their fathers'. All of these new planters would also require slaves, and the western farms would provide markets for slaves born back East. Ambitious planters settled the wildly fertile Mississippi Valley first, then filled in the passed-over places in subsequent generations.

Unwittingly, the North and South rift left unsettled in the Constitution had been projected into the western territories. The Northwest Ordinance outlawed slavery north of the Ohio River. As a result, it practically guaranteed the spread of slavery south of that line. In addition, it would turn any western expansion of the nation into a contest between the sections already coalescing on the shores of the Atlantic. Lawmakers would have to weigh each new accession of territory as to its implications for the North and South rivalry. Both sides considered western territories as part of the national patrimony, and each state considered itself heir.

For average Americans, the West was also of profound importance. The pattern of western expansion had been set with the Treaty of Paris, which ceded to the new nation all of the territory to the Mississippi River. In 1803, Jefferson advanced the national mission of acquiring new lands by consummating the Louisiana Purchase, effectively doubling the size of the United States. "It is an Empire for Liberty" he wrote, proposing that the new region would provide homes and farms for all who would have them for the next forty generations.

Inexpensive lands in the West promised social mobility, a fresh start, and the future of the nation. The West of the imagination served as a catalyst for national greatness, and as long as average citizens could move west, optimism for the nation ran high. This unfettered enthusiasm ran counter to the calculated wrangling of lawmakers concerned with sectional balance.

Not everyone was enamored of the West. As settlers moved to the frontier, they faced a host of opponents on a variety of fronts. Indians, supported with food and ammunition from British Canada and Spanish Florida, fought a proxy war with the expansionist Americans.

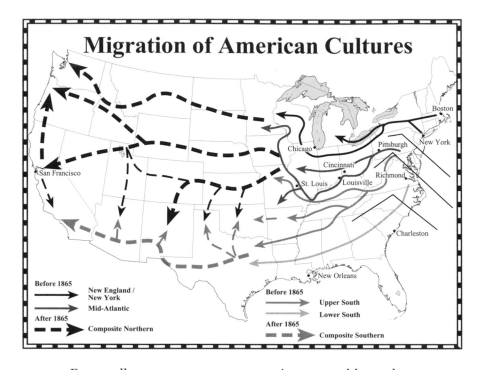

Migration of American Cultures

Eventually, concerns over western issues would greatly contribute to the War of 1812 between the United States and the British. Although ostensibly about shipping issues and sailors' rights, the U.S. goal was clearly the invasion and conquest of Canada and the annihilation of any future Indian threat—both western issues. Sensing the true nature of the war and fearing a loss of power and prestige as the nation shifted westward, a coalition of mostly New England states openly opposed the war, going so far as to trade with the enemy while whispering the word secession. The end of the war settled the issue, but in its first trial of arms as a nation, the quarrelsome nature of the country had made for a very poor showing.

By 1821 the Missouri Compromise had provided another episode for sectional squabbling. The question of slavery in the statehood debate for Missouri lay outside of the old Northwest

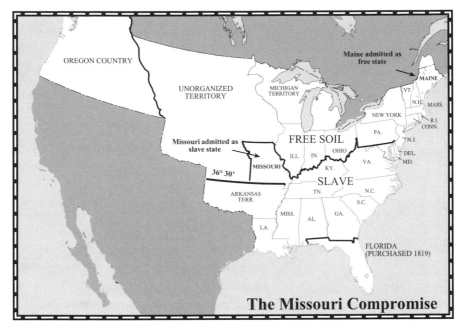

The Missouri Compromise

Ordinance rules, and was the first such unresolved issue facing the nation. Partisans North and South argued their points, and ultimately settled on an artificial boundary between free states and slave at the southern border of Missouri. As a result, two furies were unleashed.

The Federal government set itself in place as the arbitrator of the slave issue, removing that right of self-determination from the states. Secondly, slavery could expand only into lands then held by foreign powers, placing the United States onto an imperialistic, and by necessity expansionist, course. The Missouri Compromise only settled the immediate issue while further solidifying sectionalism in the nation, and it surrendered to the Federal government the power to define the legal limits of slavery.

Texas was next, and it proved to be the fruit of the Missouri Compromise. In 1821 Americans began settling in the Mexican province at the invitation of its government. By 1830 U.S. citi-

zens, current and former, had become the overwhelming majority. Two years later, these Anglo-Celtic settlers were in rebellion, and four years after that had declared their outright independence. These settlers were overwhelmingly Southerners by birth, and slavery would be part of their baggage as they wrested the land from its hereditary masters.

Nor were all of the contentious issues about expansion and territorial aggrandizement. Foreign trade issues also rocked the shaky national coalition. A high protective tariff, designed to protect and foster American industry, infuriated southern agriculturalists who saw little benefit from the policy but did realize a steady rise in consumer prices. Angry that national policy and resources could be used to favor one region over another, the politicians of South Carolina simply declared the national laws "null and void" in their state and refused enforcement.

By 1832 the Nullification Crisis pitted the issue of States Rights versus the authority of the Federal government. Although settled without bloodshed, it revealed lingering issues over the nature of the national compact and proved a precursor for political debate later in the century.

In the 1840s, a new generation of Americans yearned for their country to take its place among the world's great nations. Arguing that history had revealed that the true mission of the nation was to expand into new lands and to bring republicanism to foreign peoples, these "Young Americans" rallied behind a phrase: Manifest Destiny.

First suggested by writer John L. O'Sullivan in an article published in *The United States Democratic Review,* he wrote, "We may confidently assume that our country is destined to become the great nation of futurity." He also laid claim to an honor which subsequent history would mock. "It is our unparalleled glory that we have no reminiscences of battle fields, but in defence of humanity, of the oppressed of all nations, of the rights of conscience, the rights of personal enfranchisement," O'Sullivan continued. "Our annals describe no scenes of horrid carnage, where men were led on by hundreds of thousands to slay one another, dupes and victims to . . . demons in the human form called heroes."

In order to bring this higher civilization to the world, adherents of this national mission argued, the United States must annex Texas as well as Oregon, jointly held by the U.S. and Great Britain, and Mexican Alta California. "[It is] the right of our manifest destiny to over spread and to possess the whole of the continent which Providence has given us for the development of the great experiment of liberty," O'Sullivan trumpeted. There was no mention in their rhetoric of slavery, states rights, or other issues that had plagued the nation thus far. The eyes of "Young America" were set firmly ahead with a self-confidence built by a selective reading of their own past.

This bellicose attitude had mixed results. Great Britain, unwilling to go to war over a Pacific Coast wilderness, arrived at a diplomatic solution that split the Oregon country between the two nations. Mexico, for its part, would not go quietly. South of the Rio Grande, "independent" Texas was a farce. Instead, Mexican leaders considered that province as simply "in rebellion," following an attempt at secession. Any effort by the United States to annex Texas would be a declaration of war. It was likewise with California, and although never closely administered by Mexico City, the region was part of the Mexican nation, and any U.S. designs on it would be met with force of arms.

The resulting War with Mexico, fought from 1846-1848, was approached with an odd mix of fervent patriotism, righteous indignation, and political intrigue. While the nation and the administration of President James Knox Polk were clear on what the war was for, few could answer why.

Designed as a short, sharp engagement that would gain the desired territories, the war ground on for much longer than anticipated, allowing time for opposition groups to gather and to voice their opinions. From Massachusetts's transcendentalist writers to South Carolina proslavery politicians, angry voices of protest demanded to be heard. Most Americans, Northerners and Southerners, had a clear opinion, but generally U.S. nationalism transcended all other arguments.

By the end of the fighting, an exuberant nation gloried in its triumph. Mexico ceded more than a third of its national territory. The question arose, north of the Rio Grande, of what to do with this new territory. The American triumph, so gallantly earned in battle, would become mired in the unresolved issues of the U.S. Constitution.

By 1849, the heterogeneous collection of people who likened themselves as "These United States" had won their first war of conquest against a foreign power. The nation had spread from Atlantic to Pacific, and this seventy-three year gallop had seen an empire carved from the wilds. This same period had also witnessed mutually antagonistic cultures and economies nervously co-existing as the mission of the nation progressed.

There had been dark rumblings all along. There had been threats of disunion on many occasions, both North and South. But, through it all, the American people had worked together for the national purposes. In the coming decade, this cooperative spirit would disappear. The "Manifest Destiny" of the United States ground to a halt, jammed and frozen by the dross of unfinished national business.

> Donald S. Frazier
> President and CEO
> Grady McWhiney Research Foundation

Chapter One
A NATIONAL CRISIS

A Divided Nation. In 1849 President Zachary Taylor faced a national crisis. Thanks to the Wilmot Proviso, a bill introduced in Congress to prohibit slavery in any territory acquired from Mexico, discussions over the question of slavery's expansion ruled politics. Sectional debate dominated the 31st Congress that assembled on December 3. In the House of Representatives, surrounded by 112 Democrats and 105 Whigs, thirteen Free Soilers held the balance of power. Southern Whigs, led by Georgians Alexander H. Stephens and Robert Toombs, opposed the Whig candidate for Speaker, Robert C. Winthrop of Massachusetts, because the Whig caucus had refused to oppose the Wilmot Proviso. The Free Soilers also refused to back Winthrop, but because during his previous service as Speaker he had been too proslavery—in other words, he had failed to recognize some antislavery spokesmen. The debates, marked by threats of disunion, widened the breach between the northern and southern wings of the Whig party.

Furnaces in Full Blast. In the Senate, where the Democrats enjoyed only a majority of ten, Senator Henry Clay of Kentucky described the debate over the extension of slavery: "we have in the legislative bodies of this capitol and in the States twenty odd furnaces in full blast, emitting heat and passion and intemper-

The Mexican Cession

ance, and diffusing them throughout the whole extent of this broad land." Senator Daniel Webster of Massachusetts, who considered the situation dangerous, complained of the disputing sections throwing the "whole nation into commotion."

The Issues. Five questions—"the five bleeding wounds," as Clay called them—demanded settlement. First, should California be admitted as a free or a slave state? Second, should the Wilmot Proviso be applied or should slavery be allowed in the territories of New Mexico and Utah? Third, what should be done with Texas, which claimed a substantial portion of New Mexico and threatened trouble if its claims should be denied? Fourth, should slavery be allowed to continue in the District of Columbia, which was the center of a flourishing traffic in slaves? Dealers led slaves through the streets of Washington, and slave sales were visible from the capitol. The fifth "bleeding wound" was the inefficiency of the existing fugitive slave law, adopted in 1793.

The Fugitive Slave Law. The Supreme Court had decided in *Prigg* v. *Pennsylvania* in 1842 that the fugitive slave clause in the Constitution was exclusively a Federal power, hence no state was obliged to enforce the fugitive slave law. Northern states immediately enacted a series of "personal liberty" laws that prohibited state authorities from assisting in the return of fugitive slaves. Abolitionists frustrated slave owners with these "personal liberty" laws and the so-called "underground railroad," a secret organization that sheltered and helped fugitives reach Canada, where slavery was illegal. Southerners, therefore, demanded a new fugitive slave law, one that would enable masters to retake runaway slaves in spite of the "personal liberty" laws and "the underground railroad." Would Congress pass such a law or would slave owners have to be content with the existing statute?

Balanced Against the South. On every one of these questions opinions divided along sectional rather than party lines. It was not Whigs against Democrats, but free states against slave states, North against South. The North desired the admission of California as a free state. The South objected, because if California entered the Union as a free state there would be sixteen free states and only fifteen slave states. The balance of power between the two sections would be disturbed. "The admission of California," said John C. Calhoun, "will be the test question. If you admit her, it will be notice to us that you propose to use your present strength and to add to it with the intention of destroying irretrievably the equilibrium between the two sections."

Hemming in Slavery. But sharper than the differences over California were those over New Mexico and Utah. Slavery in those territories was already prohibited at the time of their acquisition, and the North demanded that the prohibition be made permanent. This slap in the South's face was the equivalent of saying to Southerners that not a single slave state would be carved out of the vast territory acquired from Mexico; that slavery henceforth must forever be hemmed within its present boundaries. If slaveholders were shut out of California and New Mexico and Utah, into what new land would it ever be possible for them to take their slaves?

Taylor's Plan. President Taylor offered a plan to Congress for dealing with the difficult issues that divided Northerners and Southerners. Wishing to move slowly and not to press all the issues at once, he advised the Congress that met in December 1849 to admit California and to suspend action on New Mexico and Utah until the people of these territories had framed constitutions. Southern leaders rejected this plan, for they feared that the Wilmot Proviso would be grafted into the forthcoming constitutions of New Mexico and Utah. Clay also opposed the President's policy because he believed it fell short of what the situation required. "What is the plan of the President?" asked Clay. "Is it to heal all these wounds? No such thing. It is to heal only one of the five and to leave the other four to bleed more profusely than ever by the sole admission of California." Taylor strongly urged his policy, but made little headway. Congress seemed determined to meet the crisis in its own way.

Compromise Necessary. The two houses of Congress were divided on the major questions. The majority of the House opposed the extension of slavery, while a majority of the Senate favored its extension. If there was to be action at all there must be a compromise. Senator Clay, who considered himself a Westerner, assumed the responsibility; the task was congenial to him, for he considered compromise one of the "white virtues." He favored "honorable compromise whenever it can be made," believing that "society is formed on the principle of mutual concession, politeness, comity, [and] courtesy. . . . I bow to you to-day because you bow to me. You are respectful to me because I am respectful to you. Compromises have this recommendation, that if you concede anything, you have something conceded to you in return."

Clay's Plan. In this spirit of give and take, Clay offered a set of resolutions in January 1850 that he hoped would "settle and adopt amicably all existing questions of controversy arising out of the institution of slavery, upon a fair, equitable, and just basis." The main features of Clay's plan were: first, to admit California as a free state—a concession to the North; second, to organize New Mexico and Utah as territories without restriction on slavery—a sacrifice of the Wilmot Proviso and therefore a concession to the South; third, to settle the boundary line between Texas and New Mexico by slightly favoring the demands of Texas and paying the state a money indemnity for its claims to the rest of the territory—a concession to the South; fourth, to abolish slave trading in the District of Columbia—a concession to the North; fifth, but not to abolish slavery in the district without the consent of Maryland—a concession to the South; and sixth, to enact a more stringent and effectual fugitive slave law—a concession to the South.

Debate. The debate over Clay's plan lasted from January to October 1850. William H. Seward of New York, who considered "all legislative compromises radically wrong and essentially vicious," supported the Wilmot Proviso and appealed to "a higher law" against slavery. Jefferson Davis of Mississippi advocated congressional noninterference with slavery and favored equal rights for the South. Salmon P. Chase of Ohio claimed it was Congress's duty to prohibit slavery in the territories. Clay, now in his seventy-fourth year and sometimes so ill that he could hardly drag his tottering frame to the Senate, made speech after speech in defense of his scheme.

Calhoun's Objections. Calhoun, who opposed Clay's plan, was also greatly enfeebled and too ill to speak. He appeared in the Senate, however, and had his speech read by Senator James M. Mason of Virginia. As the reading proceeded, the gaunt and haggard old man anxiously watched the effect of his words on the faces of his colleagues. He considered Clay's plan wholly unconstitutional. Congress, Calhoun contended, had no right under the Constitution to keep slavery out of California or any other territory, slavery being a domestic institution with which the federal government had nothing to do except to make regulations regarding fugitive slaves. He opposed the plan also because he believed it would be ineffectual. The South, he said, would be so highly displeased with the compromise measures that it would withdraw from the Union. He did not want secession, but he feared it. His remedy for disunion was for the North to give the South an equal right in newly acquired territory; give it an effective fugitive slave law; cease agitating the slavery question; and restore the balance of power between the North and the South by amending the Constitution to provide for two Presidents, one for each section, with each having a veto. "If you of the North will not do this," he said, "then let our Southern States separate and depart in peace."

Webster's Speech. On March 7, 1850, Daniel Webster declared himself in favor of Clay's plan. He believed the Union was in danger and that it could be saved only by compromise. "I wish to speak," he said, "not as a Massachusetts man, not as a Northern man, but as an American. I speak to-day for the preservation of the Union." Never was a speech more severely condemned by Northerners. The antislavery people considered themselves betrayed; they believed that Webster was trying to

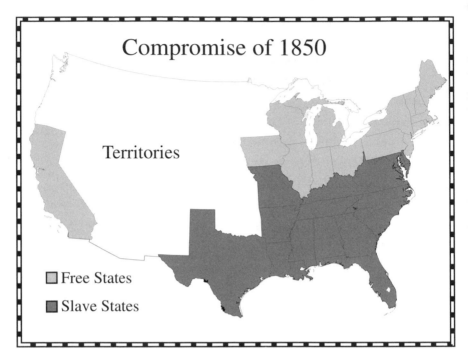

Compromise of 1850

Territories

☐ Free States
■ Slave States

curry favor with the South. "Webster is a fallen star! Lucifer descending from heaven!" announced Horace Mann. "I know no deed in American history done by a son of New England to which I can compare this but the act of Benedict Arnold," declared Theodore Parker. "The only reasonable way in which we can estimate this speech is as a bid for the Presidency."

The Omnibus Bill. As the compromise passed through the maze of legislative procedure, it was resisted at every step by President Taylor. But on July 4 Taylor, listening to speeches and walking about, overexposed himself to the sun. Upon returning to the White House, he ate some raw food and drank some cold liquids and developed a fever and inflammation of his stomach lining and intestines—what his doctors called *cholera morbus*. On July 9 he died. Vice President Millard Fillmore, who now became President, was a close friend of Clay. Fillmore made

Webster his secretary of state and threw the influence of his administration on the side of the compromise. With additional help from some Democrats led by Stephen A. Douglas of Illinois, Congress adopted the compromise. Each part was enacted separately, but by the end of September all of Clay's plan—collectively know as the Omnibus Bill, but often called the Compromise of 1850—had been passed and signed by President Fillmore.

No Finality. Politicians everywhere, North and South, did all they could to induce the people to accept the compromise measures. They proclaimed the slavery question settled and promised to execrate anyone who reopened the issue. In many cases these appeals for finality were made in all sincerity. Clay's compromise, by averting the impending crisis, brought a brief tranquility to the country, but it was an uneasy quiet. Nobody was satisfied, not even the politicians themselves. It was in vain, therefore, that leaders attempted to suppress discussion and agitation. "To be told," said James Russell Lowell, "that one ought not to agitate the question of slavery when it is that which is forever agitating us, is like telling a man with a fever and ague on him to stop shaking and he will be better."

A Harsh Law. Advocates of peace and harmony secured at least a half-hearted acceptance of the compromise in the South but not in the North. The new Fugitive Slave Law, which infuriated many Northerners, denied runaway slaves the right of trial by jury. Moreover, it excluded the testimony of blacks whose freedom was at stake; it imposed a penalty of a fine and imprisonment on any person hindering the arrest of a fugitive or aiding one to escape; it gave federal commissioners the power to pass on the merits of cases instead of leaving this power with state officials; it gave the commissioner a double fee if he determined that the service of the fugitive was due the claimant; it provided—and this was one of its most objectionable features—that any citizen might be called upon to aid in enforcing the law: "and all good citizens are hereby commanded to aid and assist in the prompt and efficient execution of this law, whenever their services may be required."

The North Revolts. Seward had warned the Senate that Northerners would not enforce the Fugitive Slave Law, and he was right. The revolt against the statute was widespread. Ralph Waldo Emerson denounced it as "a law which every one of you will break on the earliest occasion—a law which no man can obey, or abet the obeying, without loss of self-respect." Antislavery people damned the law, claiming that it was unconstitutional, immoral, abhorrent to every instinct of justice, inhuman and diabolical. The efforts of such old political leaders as Clay, Webster, Douglas, Lewis Cass, and James Buchanan to persuade the people to accept the compromise were generally successful, but in many places throughout the North their counsel was defiantly rejected.

Spreadeaglism. Politicians tried to divert attention from the slavery controversy to foreign affairs. Webster, for example, used the "Hulsemann letter" to arouse Americans. In 1849, when the Hungarians were in revolt against their Austrian masters, President Taylor had sent an agent to Vienna to watch the course of events with a view of giving recognition to the new Hungarian government, if one should be established. The American agent, A. Dudley Mann, never entered Hungary, but the offended Austrian government instructed Chevalier Hulsemann, its charge d'affaires in the United States, to register a firm protest against interference in Austrian domestic affairs. Secretary of State Webster replied in a letter defending the American right to take an interest in the extraordinary events that were occurring in Austria and other parts of Europe, and declaring that although the United States had at all times abstained from interfering with the political changes in Europe it could not fail to cherish a lively interest in nations struggling to obtain institutions similar to those of the United States. "The power of this republic," wrote Webster, "is spread over a region one of the richest and most fertile on the globe, and of an extent in comparison with which the possessions of the House of Hapsburg are but as a patch on the earth's surface." Webster acknowledged that his letter was "boastful and rough," but he excused its spreadeagle tone on the ground that he wished "to touch the national pride and make a man feel sheepish and look silly who should speak of disunion."

Kossuth. Another event that turned attention from sectionalism was the arrival of Louis Kossuth, the leader of the Hungarian revolt. After the movement for an independent Hungary had ended in failure, Kossuth came to the United States as a national guest and was received everywhere with unbounded enthusiasm. Hoping to persuade the United States to intervene in behalf of Hungary, Kossuth visited Washington, where he was received with respect and sympathy, but was disappointed. To intervene in Hungarian affairs, leaders said, would be to abandon America's policy of European non-intervention. "Far better it is for us," said Clay to Kossuth, "for Hungary, and for the cause of liberty, that, adhering to our wise and pacific system, and avoiding the distant waters of Europe, we should keep our lamp burning brightly on this western shore as a light to all nations, than to hazard its utter extinction amid the ruins of fallen and failing republics." When Kossuth left the United States in the summer of 1852, all he took with him was the country's sympathy and a small sum of money.

Franklin Pierce. While Kossuth was touring the country in behalf of Hungary, politicians were planning for the next presidential election. In 1852 the Democrats nominated Franklin Pierce of New Hampshire for President. Pierce, a man of "amiable mediocrity," was brave and handsome; his enemies were few, and his manners were graceful and winning. But his critics said in a jocular way that there was not enough positiveness in his character to enable him to refuse a drink. On the subject of slavery his views were unknown, although there was a rumor that he once said that he did not like the Fugitive Slave Law. He was, therefore, an ideal candidate for the Democrats, who went into the campaign with no positive program. The Whigs nominated Gen. Winfield Scott, preferring a military hero to the civilians, Fillmore and Webster, both of whom wanted the nomination. What Scott thought about the compromise acts was unknown, and the Whigs were careful that the public should be kept in the dark on that point. The Whigs and Democrats, indeed, vied with each other in keeping the slavery question in the background, and in affirming their entire satisfaction with the compromise measures. Consequently, the campaign was dull and listless. The Democrats tried to enliven the contest by calling Pierce "the Young Hickory of the Granite Hills" and presenting him as a new Andrew Jackson. "Young Hickory" won the election by an overwhelming majority. Scott carried only four states. It was a defeat from which the Whig party would never recover.

Old Leaders Die. Three of America's great statesmen died before the election of 1852. John C. Calhoun, who had been on his death-bed during the Compromise of 1850 debate, was the first to go; Henry Clay and Daniel Webster soon followed. All had served long and well their sections and their country; none had been President, although each had sought that office eagerly. Their contributions as cabinet members and as senators had been to offer leadership and balance, to compromise sectional issues, and to promote the nation's welfare. Now, without their guidance and counsel, the country faced extreme views and increased sectional agitation.

Chapter Two

REPEAL OF THE MISSOURI COMPROMISE

Uncle Tom's Cabin. Many people hoped that the dispute over slavery would end with the election of Pierce, but agitation continued. Millions of consciences were stirred by Harriet Beecher Stowe's *Uncle Tom's Cabin*, which appeared in book form during the campaign of 1852. The fictitious story drew an incredibly harsh picture of slavery, yet many readers found the book believable and heartbreaking. *Uncle Tom's Cabin* impressed on Northerners that slavery was cruel, brutal, and unjust. The book doubtless had little effect on the election of 1852, but thousands of impressionable boys who read it that year were voters in 1856 and 1860.

Stephen A. Douglas. Not only did such abolitionists as William Lloyd Garrison and Wendell Phillips continue their agitation, but even the more responsible leaders refused to let the subject of slavery rest. Foremost among the agitators was Stephen A. Douglas. This son of Vermont had migrated to southern Illinois, where he was admitted to the bar before he reached manhood. Ambitious almost beyond the bounds of reason, he advanced his career as fast as his restless and indomitable energy could lift him. At twenty-two he became state's attorney; at twenty-three, a member of the state legislature; at twenty-eight, a judge; at thirty, a member of the national House of Representatives; at thirty-three, a United States senator. Short—hardly five feet tall—with a head of tremendous size and great intellectual power, he became known as the Little Giant. In his manners and appearance he was grotesque, despite his affected sartorial eloquence. John Quincy Adams described Douglas speaking on the floor of House of Representatives: "His face was convulsed, his gesticulation frantic, he lashed himself into such a heat that if his body had been made of combustible matter it would have burnt out. In the midst of his roaring, to save himself from choking, he stripped off and cast away his cravat, unbuttoned his waistcoat, and had the air and aspect of a half-naked pugilist." Yet this stormy and shrewd "Little Giant" was a gifted politician.

The Nebraska Country. Douglas upset the nation by introducing a bill in the Senate in 1854 for the organization of the Nebraska country, a region comprising what are now the states of Kansas, Nebraska, North Dakota, South Dakota, Montana, and parts of Wyoming and Colorado. For some time he had been trying to secure a settled government for this "no-man's land," but Congress had refused to act. By 1854 the question of a territorial government for Nebraska had become entangled with a number of other questions—Indian titles, land grants, transcontinental railroads, and Missouri factional quarrels. What worked most strongly against the organization of Nebraska was the fact that it lay north of the parallel of 36° 30' and was, by the terms of the Missouri Compromise, closed to slavery. In western Missouri there was a vigorous proslavery party led by Senator David Atchison, which stood ready to prevent the creation of free states north of the compromise line. To meet this opposition Douglas

Kansas-Nebraska Act

Washington Territory

Oregon Territory

Nebraska Territory

Minnesota Territory

Utah Territory

Kansas Territory

New Mexico Territory

Unorganized Territory

☐ Free States and Territories

■ Slave States

▨ Voters allowed to decide whether to permit slavery

■ Territory left unorganized

proposed to divide the Nebraska country into two territories, Kansas and Nebraska, repeal the Missouri Compromise, and let the settlers in each of the new territories determine for themselves whether they would have slaves or not.

The Kansas-Nebraska Bill. This measure—known as the Kansas-Nebraska Bill—was indeed bold. To repeal the Missouri Compromise and throw open to slavery the vast region that had been closed to it was, in the minds of most Northerners, nothing less than a violation of a sacred compact. Why did Douglas make this extreme and unexpected move? Some historians believe he wanted the region organized into territories so that a railroad from St. Louis to the Pacific Coast could be built through it. "Douglas," said one authority, "was a great believer in extending the railway facilities throughout the West. To advance the railroads farther into the West they must be built through the Indian country, the title to which had to be extinguished and the land taken under government control." But this railroad theory of his motives would have failed to satisfy the Douglas's contemporaries: they believed that the senator was playing politics, and nothing else; that he had offered the bill as a bid for the support of the South in the coming election. Douglas disavowed all selfish motives. He said he knew that the bill was very unpopular, and it might end his political career, but he was prepared to follow his sense of duty and make the sacrifice.

Squatter Sovereignty. In support of his bill Douglas urged the doctrine of popular or "squatter sovereignty": the people of each territory would decide by popular vote whether or not to allow slavery. Douglas's bill declared that its true intent and meaning was "not to legislate slavery into any Territory or State, nor to exclude it therefrom, but to leave the people thereof perfectly free to form and regulate their domestic institutions in their own way." This provision, it will be recalled, was almost precisely what had been ordained for New Mexico and Utah in the Compromise of 1850.

Inoperative and Void. The Kansas-Nebraska Bill declared the Missouri Compromise "inoperative and void." Here was a gift that surprised even the proslavery men themselves, for the most ardent of them had not hoped for the repeal of the Missouri Compromise. Douglas managed his bill adroitly. When the time came to vote he was assisted by southern Democrats and Whigs and by about half of the northern Democrats. In the Senate twenty-eight Democrats and nine Whigs voted for the bill and five Democrats and seven Whigs against it. In the House forty-four northern and fifty-seven southern Democrats and twelve southern Whigs voted for the bill; against it were forty-five Whigs and forty-two Democrats from the North and two Democrats and seven Whigs from the South. The vote revealed that on the slavery question the southern Whigs were ready to break with those in the North. "What you have so long wished for," Seward wrote his wife, "has come around at last. The Whigs of the North are separated from the Whigs of the South." Thus, with the repeal of the Missouri Compromise, it appeared that Wilmot's attempt in 1846 to restrict slavery had ended in an enormous extension of territory into which Southerners might lawfully take their slaves.

The Ostend Manifesto. Proslavery leaders also hoped to annex and extend slavery to Cuba. Filibustering expeditions from the United States kept the island in constant turmoil during the early 1850s. In 1854 the American ministers to Great Britain, France, and Spain met at Ostend, Belgium, and drew up the Ostend Manifesto, declaring that Spain ought to sell Cuba to the United States; that Cuba was necessary for the safety of slavery in the South; and that, if Spain refused to sell, Cuba should be taken by force. The declaration, however, failed to secure public support in the United States, and it was strongly condemned in Europe.

Impact of Kansas-Nebraska. The Kansas-Nebraska Bill created excitement throughout the country and set in motion a train of events that led to a civil war. The immediate effect of the bill was to make the extension of slavery an overshadowing issue, one that would have to be dealt with. Hitherto there had been compromise and shuffling and evasion, but now everyone had to decide for the extension of slavery or against it. "The bill annuls all past compromises with slavery," said Senator Charles Sumner of Massachusetts, "and makes all future compromises impossible. Thus it puts freedom and slavery face to face and bids them grapple."

Resentment in the North. Sumner was right. The passage of the Kansas-Nebraska Bill marked the end of successful compromises and the beginning of a final struggle between the friends and enemies of slavery. Northerners made widespread attacks on the bill's author. Douglas said he could travel by the light of his own burning effigies from Boston to Chicago.

Antislavery displeasure assumed a variety of forms. Feeling that the repeal of the Missouri Compromise was an act of bad faith, the radical antislavery men renewed their fight against the Fugitive Slave Law. Leading citizens of Boston violently resisted attempts of United States officials to recapture slaves. In Rhode Island, Connecticut, and Michigan resistance took the form of nullification, for these states enacted personal liberty laws. These laws prohibited the retaining of fugitives in state jails; entitled blacks who were claimed as slaves to the benefit of the writ of habeas corpus and a trial by jury; and punished by fine and imprisonment attempts to seize free persons and return them to slavery. Another effect of the Kansas-Nebraska Law was to spur the abolitionists to greater activity and increase their number. "Pierce and Douglas," said Horace Greeley in 1854, "have made more abolitionists in three months than Garrison and Phillips could have made in a century." The repeal of the Missouri Compromise threw Garrison into a frenzy of dissent. He believed that the slaveholders had won a complete triumph and that the time had come for the North to break away from the South. "There is," said William Garrison's abolitionist newspaper the *Liberator*, "but one honest, straight-forward course to pursue if we would see the slave power overthrown; the Union must be dissolved." To show his disgust with constituted law and authority he publicly burned the Fugitive Slave Law and the Constitution of the United States at a meeting of abolitionists on July 4, 1854.

The Republican Party Organized. The less violent opponents of the Kansas-Nebraska Act believed that the best way to stop the advance of slavery was through political action. In

March 1854 a meeting of citizens in Ripon, Wisconsin, opposed the extension of slavery and favored starting a new party. Groups elsewhere in the North joined them to form the Republican Party. By the fall of 1854 Republicans not only had candidates running in Wisconsin, Massachusetts, Michigan, Vermont, and Maine, but had won victories in Wisconsin and Michigan. Thus within a few months after the Missouri Compromise was repealed a new party was gathering strength to resist the extension of slavery.

Bleeding Kansas. Events in the West gave the Republicans a major issue. The Kansas-Nebraska Act had made Kansas a prize to be contended for by those who favored and those who opposed slavery. "Come on then, gentlemen of the slave States!" urged Seward. "Since there is no escaping your challenge, I accept it on behalf of freedom. We will engage in competition for the virgin soil of Kansas, and God give the victory to the side that is stronger in number as it is in the right." Emigrants from Arkansas and Missouri, determined to make Kansas a slave state, soon clashed with free-state emigrants from the North. At first the slave state people had the advantage; being closer to the scene, they could cross over the Missouri line and take possession at once. But this advantage was quickly offset by the activities of the Emigrant Aid Society, which was organized in the North for the express purpose of hurrying settlers into Kansas. Most of these people were crusaders rather than pioneers seeking homes. "It is much better," said a leader of the Emigrant Aid Society, "to go and do something for free labor than to stay at home and talk of manacles and auction-blocks and bloodhounds, while deploring the never-ending aggressions of slavery." A proslavery leader responded by promising "to mark every scoundrel among you who is the least tainted with abolitionism and exterminate him. Neither give nor take quarter, as the cause demands it." Few slaveholders were willing to risk taking their slaves into such a volatile place.

The Topeka Convention. The proslavery people settled along the Missouri River, founding the towns of Atchison, Leavenworth, and Lecompton. The antislavery people made settlements along the Kansas River, their principal towns being Topeka, Lawrence, and Osawatomie. The struggle began in earnest in March 1855 following the election of a territorial legislature. The proslavery men, aided by Missourians who crossed the border to vote on election day, won control of the legislature. The antislavery people, dismissing the election as fraudulent, organized their own independent territorial government. In October 1855 at a convention in Topeka they drew up and submitted to the voters of the territory a constitution that prohibited slavery. But the proslavery men refused to participate in the voting.

Violence and Outrage. Here was an example of Douglas's "squatter sovereignty": two zealous and truculent factions, one trying to establish slavery, the other to prohibit it. Violence and outrage followed. In May 1856 the town of Lawrence was attacked by a mob of proslavery men and destroyed. In revenge, John Brown, with his four sons and three other men, went along the Pottawatomie Creek at midnight, dragged five proslavery men from their cabins, and killed them in cold blood. Fanatic that he was, Brown did this from a sense of duty; he believed that he was divinely commissioned to perform such bloody deeds. "It has been decreed," he said, "by Almighty God, ordained from all eternity, that I should make an example of these men."

He Bellowed Like a Calf. The violence in Kansas concerning the extension of slavery had its counterpart in the halls of Congress. During the angry debate over the admission of Kansas, Senator Charles Sumner of Massachusetts delivered a speech as "offensive and insulting to the South as the fertile imagination of the author could possibly make it." In his vitriolic attack on several senators, particularly the absent and aged Senator Andrew P. Butler of South Carolina, Sumner denounced the "Slave Oligarchy" and its "rape" of Kansas. The speech outraged many people and even Sumner's allies considered it too extreme. Congressman Preston Brooks of South Carolina, Butler's nephew, decided to avenge this insult to his kinsman. Brooks rejected challenging Sumner to a duel; he believed the New Englander too cowardly to fight and besides duels took place only between social equals. "To punish an insulting inferior" was all that Brooks intended; "it was expressly to avoid taking life," he explained, "that I used an ordinary cane"—a gutta-percha walking stick with a hollow core. Several days after the speech, Brooks approached Sumner at his senate desk and "gave him about 30 first rate stripes." Brooks recalled that when hit Sumner "bellowed like a calf." The affair created a tremendous sensation. The House of Representatives censured Brooks. He immediately resigned, but his district unanimously reelected him, and he received canes from all over the South. The bill that caused the trouble—the one providing for the admission of Kansas under the Topeka constitution—failed to pass. The House, with a good sprinkling of Republicans, favored the measure, but the Senate, which Southerners still controlled, voted against admission.

The Issue in 1856. The major issue of the presidential campaign of 1856 was whether Kansas should be admitted as a slave state or as a free state. Never before had there been a presidential election where the issue was so straightforward, yet never had the situation of political parties been more complicated. There were northern Whigs, southern Whigs, northern Democrats, southern Democrats, and Republicans. Whigs in the North were going over to the Republicans; Whigs in the South to the

Democrats. To add to the confusion, a third party that met secretly, was anti-immigrant and anti-Catholic, and threw around itself an atmosphere of mystery was appealing for support. Officially called the American party, but popularly known as the Know-Nothing party because its members used the password "I don't know," this organization drew support chiefly from old-line Whigs and discontented northern Democrats.

Know-Nothings. The Know-Nothings were the first to name their candidate. In February 1856 their convention met at Philadelphia and adopted a platform that denounced "the corrupting tendencies of the Roman Catholic Church" and advocated that "Americans only shall govern America." Many of the party's antislavery members withdrew when the convention refused to denounce slavery expansion. For President the convention nominated ex-President Fillmore.

The Democratic Nominee. In June the Democrats held their convention at Baltimore. Their problem was to nominate a candidate who would keep the northern Democrats faithful to their party and who would also be acceptable to the South. Either Pierce or Douglas might suit the South, because both had advocated the Kansas-Nebraska Act, but both were denied the nomination. The most available man was James Buchanan of Pennsylvania. Southerners supported him because he was a conservative Jacksonian Democrat; as ambassador to Great Britain during the Kansas controversy, Buchanan had been unobliged to take sides. Strong in Pennsylvania, a state whose electoral votes the Democrats needed, Buchanan received the nomination after much balloting. In their platform the Democrats stood by the Kansas-Nebraska Act, asserting the right of the people of the territories "to form a constitution with or without slavery."

The Republican Nominee. The Republicans by this time had a strong organization and were ready to enter the presidential race. Representatives from none of the southern but all of the northern states attended the first Republican convention in Philadelphia. There they selected as their presidential candidate John C. Fremont, a young officer who had taken an active part in the conquest of California. The platform declared that Congress should prohibit slavery in the territories and demanded the immediate admission of Kansas as a free state.

The Campaign of 1856. The election of 1856 was a contest in which passion, fueled by events in Kansas, burned fiercely. Seward stated the central issue of the campaign on the Republican side in a speech at Rochester, New York. "It is," he said, "an irrepressible conflict between opposing and enduring forces, and it means that the United States must and will, sooner or later, become either entirely a slaveholding nation or entirely a free labor nation. . . . I know and you know that a revolution has begun. I know and all the world knows that revolutions never go backward." Clergy and intellectuals throughout the North supported the Republicans, but Southerners threatened secession if the Republicans won. "The Southern States," said Virginia's governor, "will not submit to a sectional election of a Free Soiler or Black Republican." The Democrats won the election. Buchanan received 174 electoral votes; Fremont got 114. Yet the Republicans received an enormous popular vote—1,342,000 for Fremont, against 1,838,000 for Buchanan and 874,000 for Fillmore. Nearly all of the votes cast for Fremont came from the North; in the South he received virtually no votes at all. The election revealed not only that the Republican Party was a major sectional party but also that the slavery question would continue to divide the North and the South.

Chapter Three

TOWARD DISUNION

No Rest on Slavery. No sooner was James Buchanan inaugurated on March 4, 1857, than the slavery issue took on new meaning. Buchanan had hoped that the question was at rest. In his inaugural address, when touching on the legal power of the territorial inhabitants to prohibit slavery, he said: "This is happily a matter of but little practical importance. Besides, it is a judicial decision which legitimately belongs to the Supreme Court . . . , before whom it is now pending, and will . . . be speedily and finally settled." The decision to which the President referred was the case of *Dred Scott* v. *Sanford.*

The Dred Scott Case. The facts in this celebrated case were clear and simple. Scott was a slave who had been taken by his master, first to Illinois, where slavery was prohibited by the Ordinance of 1787; then to Minnesota Territory, where slavery was prohibited by the Missouri Compromise; and then to Missouri, a slave state. In Missouri, antislavery advocates brought suit in court to have Scott set free on the ground that his residence in free Illinois and free Minnesota made him a free man. His case, in the course of appeal, at last reached the Supreme Court. That tribunal's decision was handed down by Chief Justice Roger B. Taney two days after Buchanan's inauguration.

The Decision. The first question—and under ordinary procedure the only question that the court had to decide—was

States Admitted, 1845–1860

☐ Free States
■ Slave States

whether or not Scott was a citizen of the United States within the meaning of the Constitution with rightful standing in the Federal courts. To this question the court returned a flat negative: Scott, being a Negro and a descendant of slave parents, could not be a citizen of the United States and could not therefore carry his suit into a federal court. The case was accordingly dismissed for want of jurisdiction. If the court had stopped with a simple dismissal of the case little would have been heard of it. But the court did not stop there. It went on to decide whether Congress was authorized to pass the Missouri Compromise Act under any of the powers granted to it by the Constitution. To this question the court decided that Congress had no more right to prohibit slavery north of the line 36° 30' than it had to prohibit the carrying of horses or any other property into the territory north of that line. In other words, the Missouri Compromise was unconstitutional and void.

Effects of the Decision. The decision made a profound impression on the public. It undercut the Republicans. Even if they gained control of Congress they could not prevent the extension of slavery, for slavery now had a new legal aspect. Congress no longer had any power regarding either the extension or the restriction of slavery. If, after this decision, Congress should attempt to prohibit slavery in Kansas or anywhere else, whether in a state or in a territory, its actions would be void. Under the Constitution, Congress could preserve and protect slavery, but it was powerless to prohibit it. Southerners, of course, were delighted. The court's decision accorded perfectly with the doctrine of Calhoun—slavery as a domestic institution wholly beyond the federal government's power or jurisdiction. States alone could allow or disallow slavery.

The Lecompton Constitution. If Buchanan really believed that the Dred Scott decision would put slavery agitation to rest he was cruelly disappointed. He found the issue still alive and troublesome as Congress assembled in December 1857. Few slaves had been taken to Kansas, for there was no certainty that its citizens would permanently legalize slavery. Nevertheless, the proslavery men were bent on making Kansas a slave state. They met at Lecompton, drew up a constitution favoring slavery, and submitted it to the people for ratification. With the antislavery people refusing to participate in the election, the proslavery people easily ratified their constitution. In February 1858 President Buchanan recommended to Congress the admission of Kansas as a slave state. But powerful congressional politicians objected and speakers in both houses assailed the proposed constitution. Douglas denied that the Lecompton constitution represented the will of the people of Kansas; it was a fraud, he claimed.

Failure of the Lecompton Constitution. The administration brought every patronage resource and influence to bear on Congress to secure the admission of Kansas under the Lecompton constitution. Friends of the measure were successful in the Senate, but they were checked in the House. In order to break the deadlock, Congress agreed to offer Kansas a grant of public lands—if the lands were accepted by a popular vote then Kansas would be admitted to the Union with the Lecompton constitution; if the gift of lands were rejected then Kansas would not be admitted until the territory had a population of about 90,000. The lure to induce acceptance of the constitution failed. An overwhelming majority of voters rejected both the land offer and the Lecompton constitution. Kansas accordingly remained a slave territory, because the Dred Scott decision legalized slavery in Kansas and gave it the full protection of the Constitution. Thus the Lecompton controversy created several problems: it hurt Buchanan in the North and Douglas in the South, encouraged southern extremists, and gave the Republicans a powerful campaign issue.

The Lincoln-Douglas Debates. The Republicans hoped to defeat Senator Douglas, whose "squatter sovereignty" proposal had been damaged by the Dred Scott decision. When Douglas opposed the Lecompton constitution, he gravely offended the administration. Buchanan withdrew from him all federal patronage, and in many of the counties in Illinois anti-Douglas tickets were put up with the expectation of electing a legislature hostile to the senator. When Douglas faced reelection in 1858 he was forced to debate his Republican opponent, Abraham Lincoln.

Lincoln's Autobiography. Compared with his antagonist, Lincoln was an obscure man. The story of his life up to 1858 he told in his own words: "I was born February 12, 1809, in Hardin County, Kentucky. . . . My father removed from Kentucky to what is now Spencer County, Indiana, in my eighth year. . . . There I grew up. There were some schools, so called, but no qualifications were ever required of a teacher. . . . Of course when I became of age I did not know much. I have not been to school since. I was raised to farm-work, which I continued until I was twenty-two. At twenty-one I came to Illinois. . . . Then I got to New Salem, where I remained a year as a sort of clerk in a store. Then came the Black Hawk War and I was elected a captain of volunteers, which gave me more pleasure than any I have had since. I ran for the legislature the same year [1832] and was beaten, the only time I was ever beaten by the people. In 1846 I was elected to the lower house of Congress. . . . I was losing interest in politics when the repeal of the Missouri Compromise aroused me again. What I have since done is pretty well known. I am in height 6 feet 4 inches nearly, lean in flesh, weighing on an average of 180 pounds, dark complexion with coarse black hair and gray eyes."

A House Divided Against Itself. In the Lincoln-Douglas debates slavery was the central theme. Lincoln said in a speech delivered before the debate began: "I believe this government cannot endure permanently half slave and half free. I do not expect the Union to be dissolved—I do not expect the house to fall—but I do expect it will cease to be divided. It will become all one thing or all the other." When the two debaters met, Douglas attacked this "house-divided-against-itself" doctrine: "Why can't the Union endure divided against itself into free and slave States? Why can't it exist upon the same principle upon which our fathers made it? Our fathers knew when they made this government that in a country as wide and broad as this . . . the people necessarily required different local laws and local institutions. . . . One of the reserved rights of the States was that of regulating the relation between master and slave, or the slavery question. At that time—that is, when the Constitution was made—there were thirteen States in the Union, twelve of which were slave States and one was a free State. Suppose the doctrine of uniformity—all to be one or all to be the other—now preached by Mr. Lincoln, had prevailed then, what would have been the result? Of course the twelve slaveholding States would have overruled the one free State and slavery would have been fostered by a constitutional provision on every inch of the American continent, instead of being as our fathers wisely left it, each State to decide for itself."

Freeport Doctrine. During the debate at Freeport, Lincoln asked Douglas how he could reconcile the doctrine of "popular sovereignty" with the Dred Scott decision. Douglas's reply became known as the "Freeport Doctrine." He insisted that the people of a territory could, by lawful means, exclude slavery prior to the formation of a state constitution by making no laws to protect slavery. Despite the Dred Scott decision, said Douglas, "slavery cannot exist a day or an hour anywhere" without laws to protect it. Southerners denounced the "Freeport Doctrine" as a clever dodge; they dismissed Douglas as just another unreliable Yankee and denied him their support in the presidential campaign of 1860.

Lincoln on Slavery. Every aspect of the slavery issue emerged during the debate. Douglas had the advantage of education, oratorical skill, and personal magnetism. In the discussion of constitutional questions the "Little Giant" often appeared superior to his antagonist. But Lincoln won support, especially in northern Illinois, by focusing on the moral aspects of slavery. Douglas did not seem to care whether slavery was voted up or down, while Lincoln insisted that slavery was wrong. He hated slavery, he said, as much as any abolitionist. He claimed that Douglas "has the high distinction, so far as I know, of never having said slavery is either right or wrong. Almost everybody else says one or the other, but the judge never does."

Lincoln's Tolerance. Lincoln denounced slavery, but he admitted that "If all earthly power were given me, I should not know what to do as to the existing institution. . . . I have no purpose, directly or indirectly, to interfere with the institution of slavery in the States where it exists. I believe I have no lawful right to do so, and I have no inclination to do so. I have no purpose to introduce political and social equality between the white and black races. . . . But I hold that . . . there is no reason in the world why the negro is not entitled to all the natural rights enumerated in the Declaration of Independence—the right to life, liberty, and the pursuit of happiness. . . . He is my equal and the equal of Judge Douglas, and the equal of every living man."

Results of the Debate. Douglas achieved a great personal triumph following the debate, but his victory had small political significance. He secured a majority in the legislature and thus won the senatorship, for senators at that time were elected by the state legislatures. The combined vote of the various candidates favorable to Lincoln was 190,000 as against 174,000 for the avowed Douglas candidates, but Douglas had the advantage of twelve holdover Democratic state senators. When the legislature met in January, Douglas got fifty-four votes; Lincoln got forty-six. The most important result of the debate was that it presented the clearest expression of the Republican position on slavery and it brought Lincoln to the attention of the country, for the contest was watched with nationwide interest and the speeches were published in many leading newspapers. By the time the debate ended Lincoln had added to his political reputation.

John Brown's Raid. Events constantly widened the gulf between the North and the South. The excitement aroused by the Lincoln-Douglas debates was followed by an episode that stirred the nation. This was a raid led by the fanatical John Brown, who earlier had been engaged in the Kansas struggle. For the purpose of inciting slaves to rebel against their masters, Brown obtained money from a number of New England and New York abolitionists. He hoped to instigate a slave insurrection in Virginia, establish a free state in the southern Appalachians, and spread a servile rebellion southward. On the night of October 19, 1859, he marched into Virginia with about twenty companions and seized the federal arsenal at Harpers Ferry. He managed to terrorize the village for a few hours, but failed in his efforts to stir any slaves to insurrection. A few men on both sides died in the fighting; the mayor of the village was shot, and two of Brown's sons lost their lives. A small force of marines commanded by Col. Robert E. Lee quickly surrounded the insurgents. Advised to surrender, Brown refused. "I prefer to die just here," he announced, but Brown and his surviving followers were taken prisoner. "We are abolitionists from the North, come to take and release your slaves," he admitted when questioned. After a trial in the county court, he was convicted of treason and murder and hanged.

Crown of Martyrdom. The raid was a miserable failure and in itself a small affair, but it created a tremendous sensation. A spasm of terror engulfed the South. When the news spread that an attempt had been made to rouse and arm the slaves, indignant citizens demanded vengeance. In the antislavery circles of the North, Brown's lawlessness was both ignored and forgiven, and the old man received the crown of martyrdom. Ralph Waldo Emerson, speaking to a Boston audience, called Brown a "new saint . . . whom none purer or more brave was ever led by love of men into conflict and death—the new saint awaiting his martyrdom, and who, if he shall suffer, will make the gallows glorious like the cross." An immense concourse of New Englanders responded enthusiastically to this sentiment.

The Impending Crisis. A scathing denunciation of slavery by Hinton R. Helper of North Carolina added to the excitement caused by Brown's raid. Helper's book, *The Impending Crisis,* which sympathized more with poor whites than with slaves, argued that slavery depressed and degraded poor Southerners and enabled slave owners to profit at the plain folk's expense. Helper presented an imposing array of statistics to show that slavery was unsound from an economic point of view. He insisted that the abolition of slavery would improve the material interests of the South and that the plain folk would share in the prosperity. Although a Southerner, Helper earned the bitter condemnation of the slaveholders. One congressman claimed that *The Impending Crisis* fostered "riots, treason, and insurrection, and is in precisely the spirit of the act which startled us a few weeks since at Harpers Ferry." In the South efforts were made to prevent the book's sale.

Democrats Split in 1860. The Dred Scott decision, the great debate in Illinois, Bloody Kansas, John Brown's raid, and Helper's book all worked together to focus attention on the slavery question, which sundered the Democratic party and became the paramount issue in the election of 1860. When the national convention assembled at Charleston, South Carolina, two factions struggled violently for control—northern Democrats and southern Democrats. The northern Democrats wanted Douglas as their candidate, but Southerners distrusted the "Little Giant." In the debate with Lincoln he had said that the people had the right to make Kansas either a slave territory or a free territory. This position had strengthened him in the North, for northern Democrats stood firm for the principle of "squatter sovereignty." But southern Democrats stood just as firm for the doctrine laid down in the Dred Scott decision, a doctrine formulated in their platform in the following words: "Neither *Congress* nor a *Territorial* legislature . . . possesses the power to annul or impair the constitutional right of any citizen of the United States to take his slave property into the common Territories and there hold and enjoy the same while the Territorial conditions remain." William L. Yancey of Alabama charged that the rise of the Republican Party was due to pandering by the Democratic Party in the free states to antislavery sentiments. "If," he said, "you had taken the position directly that slavery was right and therefore ought to be, you would have triumphed and antislavery would now have been dead in your midst." The demand that northern Democrats say that slavery was right was more than some of them could stand.

Two Platforms and Two Nominees. The proceedings of the convention soon disclosed fatal dissensions both regarding the adoption of a platform and the nomination of candidates. When defeated upon a resolution embodying the doctrine of the Dred Scott decision, most southern delegates protested and withdrew. As it was now impossible to nominate a candidate under the two-thirds rule, the convention adjourned to meet in Baltimore in June. In the meantime the withdrawn southern delegates met in another hall in Charleston and drew up a platform to their liking. When the regular convention reassembled in Baltimore an effort was made to secure harmony, but in vain. Two Democratic tickets entered the field. The southern Democrats nominated John C. Breckinridge of Kentucky and declared that neither Congress nor a territorial legislature had the right to abolish slavery in a territory. The northern Democrats nominated Douglas and declared for popular sovereignty. Thus the Democratic Party, which had always been a compact national organization, became two sectional factions. Leaders were not blind to the meaning of the division. "Men will be cutting one another's throats in a little while," warned Alexander H. Stephens of Georgia. "In less than twelve months we shall be in a war."

Lincoln is Nominated. Encouraged by the dissension in the ranks of the opposition, the Republicans entered the campaign confident of success. They held their convention in Chicago in May. Their platform promised not to interfere with slavery in states where it already existed; repudiated the Dred Scott decision as a "dangerous political heresy"; favored a protective tariff; and demanded federal aid for the construction of a railroad to the Pacific. At the convention's outset the most prominent candidate for the nomination was William H. Seward of New York. But he had many enemies and, as the prospect of Republican success was bright, competition was fierce. On the third ballot Abraham Lincoln won the nomination.

The Constitutional Union Party. Several weeks before Lincoln's nomination, a new political group composed of conservatives who were unwilling to align themselves with either the Democrats or the Republicans met and selected a candidate. Calling themselves Constitutional Unionists, they nominated John Bell of Tennessee and declared for "the Constitution of the Country, the Union of the States, and the enforcement of the laws."

The Campaign of 1860. The campaign that followed was the most important political contest in American history. The issues were clearly defined, and the voters knew precisely what they were called upon to decide. They were to vote either for the extension of slavery or for its restriction. The campaign was serious but unexciting; few national contests were fought where the discussion was more temperate. There was no Clay, no Jackson, no Tippecanoe to excite the voters. Efforts were made to impress the great mass of doubtful voters by the force of argument. Yet it was an intense campaign. The number of speeches exceeded those made in all the previous presidential canvasses between 1789 and 1856.

Lincoln's Election. Sectionalism dominated the campaign. Of the four parties in the field not one had shown itself to be national. The Republicans carried every state north of the Mason-Dixon Line except three of the electoral votes in New Jersey, but were unsuccessful in every southern state. The southern Democrats carried all the southern states except Virginia, Tennessee, and Kentucky; these went to Bell. Douglas won only Missouri and three electoral votes in New Jersey. Lincoln received 180 of the electoral votes against 123 cast for all the other candidates combined. But he failed to obtain a majority of the popular votes, getting only 1,857,610 votes to 2,787,780 for the other three candidates—Douglas, 1,291,574; Breckinridge, 850,082; Bell, 646,124.

Chapter Four

THE CALL TO ARMS

Secession and the South. Lincoln's election united the South. Secession began immediately after the November 1860 presidential contest and by the time Lincoln became chief executive in March 1861, seven southern states had withdrawn from the Union. War soon followed, and four additional states joined the Confederacy.

The South's Power Loss. Southerners believed that the election of Lincoln deprived the South of the power to protect itself. They knew that after March 4, 1861, the presidency and all administrative officers of the Federal government would be controlled by a political party determined both to block the policies and desires of the South and to undermine its social and economic structure. This new political situation frightened them. For many years the South had been holding its own against the North by balancing slave states against free states in the Senate. But as the country expanded the scales became uneven. Since the admission of Texas in 1845 not a single slave state had entered the Union, but between 1845 and 1860 Iowa, Wisconsin, California, Minnesota, and Oregon had all come in as free states. The South's power thus had been gradually slipping away before 1860, and Southerners now interpreted Lincoln's election as the disappearance of their own power.

Road to Secession. Southerners believed that without the power to protect themselves within the Union their only hope was to secede. Long before Lincoln's election they had contemplated separation from the Union; indeed, Calhoun had preferred secession to the Compromise of 1850. In 1856 Senator Robert Toombs of Georgia wrote: "The election of Fremont would be the end of the Union and ought to be. The object of Fremont's friends is the conquest of the South. I am content that they shall own us when they conquer us, but not before." James Buchanan explained privately during the presidential campaign of 1856 "that all incidental questions are comparatively of little importance . . . when compared with the grand and appalling issue of union or disunion." Buchanan's election did nothing to settle the issue; on the contrary, the breach widened. The failure of the Lecompton Constitution, John Brown's raid, the publication of Helper's book, and the split in the Democratic convention at Charleston all worked to convince Southerners that their only course was "immediate, absolute, eternal separation." Thus, with sentiment being favorable toward secession, the South found it easy to take the final step. The election of Lincoln acted as a signal to secede, for many southern leaders had resolved to leave the Union the moment they saw no hope of the South receiving fair treatment.

South Carolina Leads the Way. The first acts of secession were prompt, swift, and decisive. South Carolina rushed headlong into the adventure. On the day after the national election the palmetto flag flew over Charleston, and on December 20, 1860, a convention of delegates dissolved the union existing between South Carolina and the other states. South Carolinians argued that they had entered into a *compact* with the other states because at the time such a union had been advantageous to all concerned, but now the other states had broken that compact, making it a burden rather than an asset to South Carolina. South Carolinians felt the personal-liberty laws enacted by northern states were destructive of the slaveholders' rights under the Constitution. Citizens of South Carolina thought non-slaveholding states had elected to the presidency a man whose opinions and purposes were hostile to slavery, and after March 4, 1861, the Federal government would be the enemy of the slaveholding states, Constitutional guarantees would no longer exist, and the equal rights of the states would be lost. South Carolina appealed to the other slaveholding states to join in forming a Confederacy. By February 1, six states of the Deep South—Mississippi, Florida, Alabama, Georgia, Louisiana, and Texas—had responded to the appeal by leaving the Union.

Why the South Seceded. The leaders of the seceding states had no doubt that they had acted in accordance with high principles and justice. Few Southerners questioned the right to secede. Like South Carolinians, they believed that the new national rulers were planning to destroy slavery and thus deprive Southerners of their constitutional rights. "We cannot close our eyes to the fact," Douglas told the Senate in January 1861, "that the Southern people have received the result of that election [of 1860] as furnishing conclusive evidence that the dominant party of the North, which is soon to take possession of the Federal Government, are determined to invade and destroy their constitutional rights. Believing that their domestic institutions, their hearthstones, and their family altars are all to be assailed, . . . and that the Federal Government is to be used for the inauguration of a . . . policy which shall have for its object the ultimate extinction of slavery in all the States—old as well as new, South as well as North—the Southern people are prepared to rush wildly, madly, as I think, into revolution, disunion, war—and defy the consequences."

The Confederate States of America. No sooner had the seceding states withdrawn from the old Union than they formed a new one. Delegates from the seceded states met on February 4 at Montgomery, Alabama, to draw up a constitution for the government of a new republic to be known as the Confederate States of America. Georgia delegate Alexander H. Stephens called this convention "the ablest, soberest, most intelligent, and conservative body I was ever in. . . . Nobody looking on would ever take this congress for a set of revolutionists." The constitution adopted for the Confederate States stated in the plainest terms the doctrine of state sovereignty and recognized slavery as a lawful institution. Although the Confederate Constitution was quite similar to the United States Constitution, there were some important differences in the two documents. The Constitution of the Confederacy forbade the enactment of a protective tariff and the importation of slaves from abroad; it gave the President a term of six years, but made him ineligible for reelection; and it allowed department heads to sit in either house of Congress and to discuss any measure affecting their department.

Preparing for War. During his inaugural on February 14 at the Confederacy's first capital in Montgomery, Alabama, Jefferson Davis declared: "there can be no cause to doubt that the courage and patriotism of the people of the Confederate States will be found equal to any measure of defense which honor and security may require." In other words, if there was fighting to be done the South would give a good account of itself. Davis wanted no war, but he feared that the North would refuse to allow the South to withdraw without a fight. The new Confederate Congress resolved that by either negotiation or force "immediate steps should be taken to obtain possession" of those forts in the South still occupied by Federal soldiers. These included Fort Sumter in Charleston harbor and Fort Pickens near Pensacola, Florida.

Federal Response. President Buchanan, Lincoln's predecessor, refused to take steps that might commit the incoming Republican administration to a fixed policy or bring on a war. In his message to Congress in December 1860, Buchanan characterized the secession movement as revolutionary, but he believed that the Federal government was powerless to force a seceding state back into the Union.

Star of the West. While Buchanan pursued a cautious policy, the secessionists acted. South Carolina took possession of all the military works near Charleston except Fort Sumter, which remained under the command of Maj. Robert Anderson. A supply ship, the *Star of the West,* tried to enter Charleston harbor and reprovision the fort on January 3, 1861, but Confederate fire compelled it to turn back. When Buchanan took no counteraction, critics condemned him severely. But he had a Congress that was still trying to resolve the situation by compromise and if he had resorted to Jacksonian methods Congress probably would have blocked him. In any event, Buchanan seemed determined that if war came, the Republicans would have to start it.

Sentiment for Compromise. For months, then, the Federal government neither countenanced secession nor favored coercion of the South. Northern public opinion seemed clearly to favor some sort of compromise to save the Union. Of the many plans offered, the proposal by Senator John J. Crittenden of Kentucky received the widest support. He suggested amending the Constitution to prohibit slavery north of parallel 36° 30' and permit it south of that line. The proposed compromise, if adopted, would have removed from slaveholders their right under the Dred Scott decision to take slaves into new states north of the Missouri Compromise line, but it would have protected their right to hold slaves south of that line.

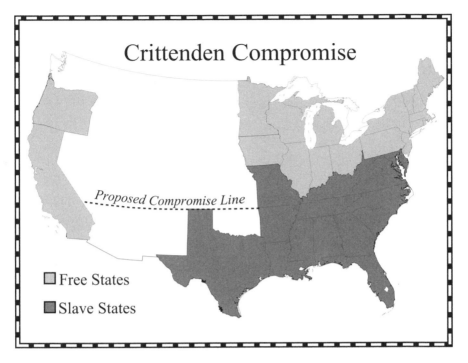

Crittenden Compromise

Proposed Compromise Line

☐ Free States
■ Slave States

Republicans Reject Compromise. Petitions favoring Crittenden's plan poured in from all parts of the country, but the Republicans in Congress were in no mood to compromise. With them, slavery was a moral issue. Many Republicans considered slaveholding a sin and slaveholders sinners, and such righteous men wanted no compromises with sinners. Southerners, on the other hand, resented being depicted as moral outcasts. The result was that in Congress ill feelings increased between the representatives of the two sections. Northerners and Southerners treated each other with mutual contempt and distrust. "So far as I know," said a senator in 1860, "every man in both houses [of Congress] is armed with a revolver and a bowie-knife." Crittenden's plan aroused such disagreement within the Senate committee considering it that the proposed amendment was never sent to the states for ratification.

No Popular Vote. After the Senate committee's failure to act, Crittenden tried another way of getting his compromise before the country. He asked that "provision be made by law, without delay, for taking the sense of the people and submitting to their vote." But again he was thwarted; Congress refused to put his compromise proposal to the people for a vote. "There can be no doubt," insisted a Richmond newspaper in January 1861, "that Crittenden's plan of adjustment, if submitted to a direct vote of the people, would be adopted by such a vote as never was polled in this country." But the Republicans, a minority party that circumstances had elevated to national power, had nothing to gain from a compromise that might reunite the Democrats.

No Compromise. However conciliatory the temper of the electorate, the attitude of northern and southern leaders made a middle course impossible. "I am daily becoming more confirmed," a congressman wrote late in 1860, "that all efforts to save the Union will be unavailing. The truth is our leaders and public men do not desire to continue it on any terms. They do not wish any redress of wrongs; they are disunionists *per se*." After the election of Lincoln not only the fire-eaters of the South but the moderate men as well were convinced that the only settlement possible was separation. Nor were northern leaders generally conciliatory. Progress might have been possible had Lincoln supported compromise, but he wrote Seward: "I am inflexible. I am for no compromise which assists or permits the extension of the institution [of slavery] on soil owned by the nation." In taking this stand Lincoln was not just upholding the main plank in the platform of the party that had elected him, but was also closing the door of hope on the Crittenden Compromise, the only conciliatory proposition that had obtained much popular support. Brought up again in the Senate on March 2, two days before Congress ended, Crittenden's proposal provoked a debate that continued into the morning of March 3. But without Republican support, the last hope of compromise perished. Now the seceding states would either depart in peace or there would be war. In just a few hours the man who would decide the outcome would become the head of government.

Chapter Five

THE CLASH
OF ARMS

Lincoln's Inaugural. Lincoln devoted his inaugural to the situation in the South. His address focused on the question raised by the seceding states and announced the policy of the incoming administration. "Apprehension seems to exist among the people of the Southern States that by the accession of a Republican administration their property and their peace and personal security are to be endangered," he stated. "There has never been any reasonable cause for such apprehension." He insisted that he had "no purpose, directly or indirectly, to interfere with the institution of slavery in the States where it exists." But he announced that "the Union of these States is perpetual," and he supported the tyranny of the majority by asserting that one state might break a contract but it required "all to lawfully rescind it." Therefore, he contended, "no State upon its own mere motion can lawfully get out of the Union."

Lincoln was determined "to hold, occupy, and possess the property and places belonging to the Government and to collect the duties and imposts; but beyond what may be necessary for these objects, there will be no invasion, no using of force against or among the people anywhere." Having promised to follow a peaceful course, he then shaded his promise by adding "unless current events and experience shall show a modification or change to be proper."

Lincoln ended by blaming Southerners for creating the crisis. "In *your* hands, my dissatisfied fellow-countrymen, and not in *mine*," he insisted, "is the momentous issue of civil war. The Government will not assail *you*. You can have no conflict without being yourselves the aggressors."

Civil War Must Now Come. The words of Lincoln, although apparently peaceful, were as threatening as low thunder. If he would not allow the seceding states to remain out of the Union—if he planned to execute the laws of the United States on the soil of the Confederate States, taking possession of southern ports, and collecting taxes at those ports—he was going to have war. If he undertook such things he was certain to be resisted, and when resistance was offered force would have to be met with force. To the country at large, and especially to the Confederacy, Lincoln's address meant war. A Richmond newspaper declared that the policy indicated by Lincoln would meet with the stern resistance of a united South, while another exclaimed: "Civil war must now come. Virginia must fight." After Lincoln's speech, the price of stock on Wall Street dropped. "We all put the same construction on the inaugural," concluded a Confederate leader. "We agreed that it was Lincoln's purpose at once to attempt the collection of the revenue, to reinforce and hold Forts Sumter and Pickens and retake the other places. He is a man of will and firmness."

Lincoln's Advisors. Throughout March, Lincoln proceeded cautiously, while he sought advice from his cabinet. He expected their suggestions to be diverse, for his cabinet consisted of prominent and competitive men: Secretary of State William H. Seward of New York, Secretary of the Treasury Salmon P. Chase of Ohio, Secretary of War Simon Cameron of Pennsylvania, Secretary of the Navy Gideon Welles of Connecticut, Secretary of the Interior Caleb B. Smith of Indiana, Attorney General Edward Bates of Missouri, and Postmaster General Montgomery Blair of Maryland. Cameron, Chase, and Welles were former Democrats, while Blair was by no means an out-and-out Republican. When reminded of the background of these men, Lincoln replied: "You seem to forget that I expect to be there, and counting me as one, you see how nicely the cabinet would be balanced. Besides, General Cameron is not Democratic enough to hurt him." It was soon discovered that Cameron—a spoilsman who had sought control of the treasury but was given instead the war office because Lincoln owed him a favor—ran a corrupt War Department. Removed in January 1862 after the discovery of widespread fraud in army contracts, Cameron was replaced by Edwin M. Stanton, a sadistic man of fierce patriotism, who managed to work well with Lincoln.

Lincoln and Fort Sumter. The cabinet and the country soon witnessed the President's skill. Southerners demanded that the sparsely provisioned Federal garrison surrender Fort Sumter, which was within range of Confederate shore batteries. Lincoln, who opposed giving up the fort, asked the head of the Federal army, Gen. Winfield Scott, for advice. "Say to the seceded States—wayward Sisters, depart in peace," suggested the aged commander. That was not what Lincoln wanted to hear, so he asked each member of his cabinet: "Assuming it to be possible to now provision Fort Sumter, under all the circumstances, is it wise to attempt it?" Seward, Cameron, Welles, Smith, and Bates said no; only Chase and Blair said yes. Seward, still hoping for conciliation, thought that a quiet evacuation of Sumter would strengthen Union sentiment in the South, allay popular excitement, and bring the seceding states back into the Union. Many people agreed with Seward. In the Senate, which was in extra session, Douglas declared on March 15 that peace was the only policy that could save the country or the Republican Party, and that the withdrawal of Major Anderson was demanded by "duty, honor, patriotism, and humanity." But Lincoln failed to see things that way. He had decided to force the Confederates into becoming the aggressors.

The Fall of Fort Sumter. An informal truce between Confederates and Federals at both Fort Sumter and Fort Pickens had prevented fighting at either, but soon after Lincoln's inauguration both presidents decided to ignore the truce. Lincoln ordered the landing of reinforcements at Fort Pickens, and Davis directed Confederate forces to capture the fort. Only after the Confederate commander at Pensacola, Gen. Braxton Bragg, decided that he might be unsuccessful in attacking Fort Pickens did Davis turn his full attention to Fort Sumter. Lincoln, after violating the truce by reinforcing Fort Pickens, decided to force Davis's hand at Fort Sumter. He informed the Confederate President that supplies—no guns, just food for hungry men—were on their way to Fort Sumter. Now Davis had the full responsibility of deciding how to react. Concluding that the fort must be captured before it could be reprovisioned, he ordered the Confederate commander at Charleston, Gen. P.G.T. Beauregard, to demand evacuation of the fort and "if this is refused proceed, in such manner as you may determine, to reduce it." Anderson refused to evacuate Fort Sumter, and on April 12, 1861, the bombardment began. Since the fort contained only sixty-four men and little ammunition, it was quickly and easily reduced. On April 13 Anderson surrendered, received permission to salute the flag as it was hauled down, and marched out with colors flying. There had been a great deal of firing during the engagement, but no loss of life on either side.

The Southern States

Responsibility for War. The first shot had been fired because neither Lincoln nor Davis tried very hard to avoid a collision. Lincoln had no desire to shoot first, but he was determined to hold the forts, and he readily broke the informal truce established under Buchanan. Davis, too, had little regard for the truce agreement. He supported it only when it seemed advantageous. Thus war came at Fort Sumter because the Confederates were neither subtle enough nor strong enough to start it at Fort Pickens.

Border States. During the first months of the secession movement eight of the slave states, loosely known as "border states"—Delaware, Maryland, Virginia, North Carolina, Kentucky, Tennessee, Arkansas, and Missouri—remained undecided on what course to follow. The allegiance of these states was vital; if they joined the Confederacy, it would have fifteen states, and its domain would exceed in area the settled portion of those states remaining in the Union. Several of the doubtful states adopted a policy of watchful waiting—they would stay in the

Union as long as there was peace, but at the opening shot they intended to join the Confederacy. "I will tell you," said Roger H. Pryor of Virginia on April 10, "what will put Virginia in the Southern Confederacy in less than an hour—strike a blow." He understood the situation. Two days later the bombardment of Fort Sumter decided the course of the border states. In Delaware the prevailing sentiment was for the Union, and there was no secession. Maryland contained a powerful secession element, but when the test came the state decided not to go out. In Virginia the governor, reacting to popular sentiment, flatly refused Lincoln's call for troops. Two days later, a convention of Virginia delegates adopted an ordinance of secession by a vote of 103 to forty-six. Arkansas followed on May 6, North Carolina on May 20, and Tennessee on June 24. Kentucky remained in the Union although it tried to pursue a course of neutrality. Missouri, which contained many secessionists, also remained in the Union. So four of the border states stayed in the Union and four went over to the Confederacy.

Unprepared. Lincoln, who had maneuvered the Confederates into firing the first shot, was prepared in mind and purpose for the conflict, but the country was not. It was the boast and the pride of the nation that its standing army was small—only about 13,000 men, scattered at military posts mostly along the frontier.

Creating Armies. The first soldiers to join the army on each side were volunteers, furnished by the states in response to calls made by the respective presidents. They came freely, men of high quality, in a period of great enthusiasm. The response to Lincoln's call for 75,000 volunteers from native-born Americans as well as immigrants showed that Fort Sumter had aroused the country. Within twenty-four hours the Sixth Massachusetts Regiment mustered in Boston Common and started south. A few days later the Seventh New York was on its way to Washington. By July 1, 1861, more than 300,000 men had joined the Federal service. Southerners responded to the call for volunteers as enthusiastically as Northerners. "The anxiety among our citizens," said Howell Cobb of Georgia, "is not who shall go to the war, but who shall stay at home." The rich, the poor, the learned, and the ignorant all went out to fight for their country and their rights. "Indeed," said a scholar, "it is doubtful that any people ever went to war with greater enthusiasm than did Confederates in 1861." By July more than 150,000 were under arms.

Conscription. But ardor eventually cooled, and by 1862 volunteering had slowed in the South as well as the North. The Confederacy enacted a Conscription Act in April 1862 that drafted into military service for three years every white man between the age of eighteen and thirty-five. Some Southerners, who denounced conscription as unconstitutional, believed that the law exempting from service men in a long list of occupations and allowing draftees to buy substitutes created "a rich man's war and a poor man's fight." Conscription in the North, which began in 1863, was equally unpopular, especially among the poor. Drafted Northerners might either buy their way out of service for $300 or furnish a substitute. The first draft in July 1863 provoked riots in New York City, where firebrands killed or injured more than 1,000 people, lynched a number of blacks, and destroyed $1,500,000 worth of private property before Federal regiments restored order.

Bounty Jumpers. The Federals used various means to obtain soldiers as the war became more destructive and fewer men volunteered. Besides making every effort to recruit newly arrived foreigners, the North offered large bounties to stimulate enlistment, which encouraged "bounty jumpers." These were men who deserted as soon as they received their bounties and enlist-

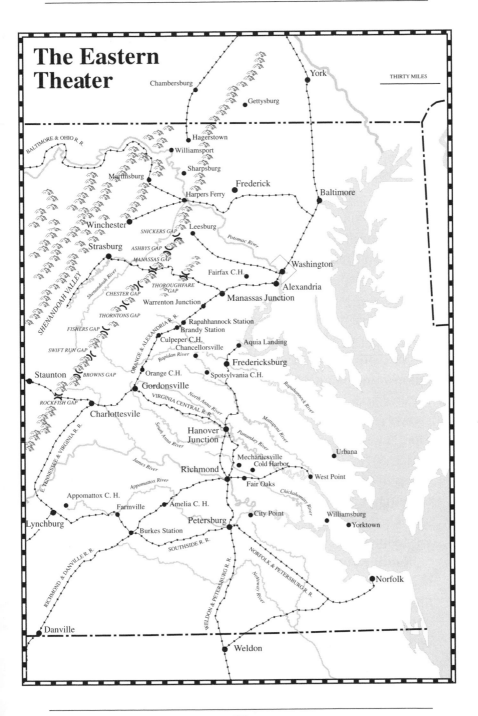

The Eastern Theater

THIRTY MILES

ed elsewhere under other names. In one case a man "jumped" his bounty thirty-two times. The enlistment of foreigners and the use of bounties led to the charge that the Federals recruited European mercenaries.

Encounter in Baltimore. As states joined or rejected the Confederacy, the border country became a battleground. The first blood was shed in Baltimore. On April 19, five days after the fall of Fort Sumter, a group of secessionists attacked the Sixth Massachusetts Regiment as it marched through Baltimore on its way to Washington. An exchange of shots killed several soldiers and citizens. The regiment fought its way to the railroad station and within a few hours reached Washington, where it was anxiously awaited by Lincoln, who was afraid southern troops might at any moment attack the capital.

West Virginia. The first skirmish between organized troops occurred in what is now West Virginia. While the eastern part of Virginia strongly favored secession the western part remained unionist. When Virginia seceded on April 17, the people over the mountains refused to go along. They took steps at once to secede from Virginia and to form a government of their own. The Confederates rushed troops into western Virginia, but in July 1861 Federal forces under Gen. George B. McClellan defeated them in a series of engagements. The people of western Virginia, pushing forward their plan of separation, organized a new state that in 1863 was admitted into the Union as West Virginia.

Kentucky and Missouri. There also were early clashes between the friends and enemies of secession in Kentucky and Missouri. The governor of Missouri, a determined secessionist, attempted to take his state out of the Union, but in battles at Wilson's Creek, Missouri, in August 1861 and at Pea Ridge, Arkansas, in March 1862 Union forces gained control of Missouri. Kentucky tried to remain neutral, but when Confederate forces crossed from Tennessee, Federal troops moved in to occupy the state. Missouri and Kentucky furnished soldiers to both sides.

American Indians. American Indians also joined both sides. Confederate Gen. Stand Watie was the only Indian general on either side during the war and the last Confederate general to surrender to Union forces. Battles in which Indians participated have received less attention than most Civil War actions, but frequently they were deadly affairs that pitted Indian against Indian, and often, tribal members against each other. The first clash of northern and southern armies in Indian Territory involved Union loyalist Creeks against Confederate Choctaws and Cherokees. One of the battles in which Indians dominated the action occurred on September 30, 1862, at Newtonia, Missouri, where 2,000 Federals attacked 500 Confederates. As the Rebels retreated, Col. Tandy Walker's First Choctaw and Chickasaw Mounted Rifles arrived at a full gallop. With fierce war cries, they charged into the Federals. The Ninth Wisconsin Infantry fled in panic, losing most of its men. Walker's troops, by their timely arrival and bold assault, "saved the day and turned the tide." Other Confederates joined in chasing the Sixth Kansas Cavalry and the Ninth Wisconsin Infantry more than five miles. It was, as one authority noted, "one of the great moments in the history of the Confederate Indians."

Manassas (Bull Run). But the battle that first excited the nation happened in 1861 in Virginia. It was called Manassas by the Confederates, who tended to name battles after towns, and Bull Run by the Federals, who frequently named them after nearby streams or bodies of water. The action took place near the Manassas Junction railroad station, located on Bull Run, about twenty-five miles southwest of Washington. Lincoln's call

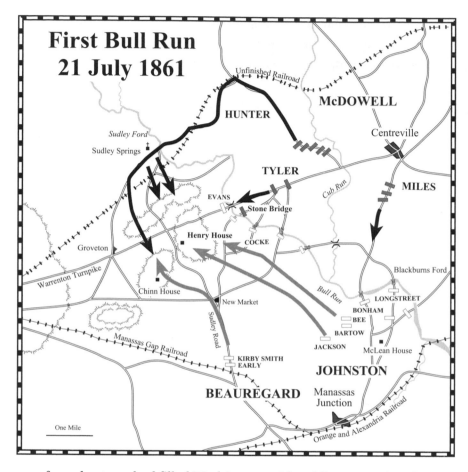

First Bull Run
21 July 1861

Unfinished Railroad

McDOWELL

HUNTER

Sudley Ford
Sudley Springs

Centreville

TYLER

Cub Run

MILES

EVANS
Stone Bridge

COCKE

Henry House

Groveton

Warrenton Turnpike

Chinn House

New Market

Sudley Road

Blackburns Ford

Bull Run

LONGSTREET
BONHAM
BEE
BARTOW
JACKSON

McLean House

Manassas Gap Railroad

KIRBY SMITH
EARLY

JOHNSTON

BEAUREGARD

Manassas
Junction

Orange and Alexandria Railroad

One Mile

for volunteers had filled Washington with soldiers, securing the nation's capital, but soon newspapers demanded that the Federal army advance on Richmond, which became the Confederate capital after Virginia seceded. "On to Richmond!" cried impatient Northerners. To please the people, but against the advice of General Scott, Lincoln decided to take action. He sent 30,000 men commanded by Gen. Irwin McDowell to attack a Confederate army under General Beauregard stationed along Bull Run. While McDowell attacked at Manassas, another Federal force was supposed to prevent Gen. Joseph E. Johnston's Confederate army in the Shenandoah Valley from reinforcing Beauregard. But Johnston managed to slip away and rushed to Beauregard's support in time to stop an initially successful Federal attack on July 21, 1861. As Johnston's men arrived by rail from the valley, Beauregard counterattacked and routed McDowell's forces, which retreated back toward the Federal capital. Confederate reinforcements might have taken Washington that night, but none were available. The Rebels were almost as disorganized in victory as the Federals were in defeat. The battle cost McDowell 2,700 of his 30,000 men in casualties; Beauregard and Johnston lost from their combined force of 32,000 men about 1,900.

The Young Napoleon. Northerners hung their heads in shame after learning that the Federals had been routed in their first important trial of strength. But Lincoln knew that defeat was due to inadequate training and bad management, and he at once set about making changes. The day after Manassas he named General McClellan commander of all forces in and around Washington. "The Young Napoleon"—as McClellan was called—was skilled at organizing and disciplining armies. The situation required all of his talent, for almost nothing had been done to train the raw regiments that were flocking into the capital. Officers lounged around the city; indeed, before McClellan took command a local joke had a boy throwing a rock at a dog on Pennsylvania Avenue and hitting three generals. But soon generals and officers were not so numerous on the streets; the new army commander kept them busy drilling and preparing their men for battle. As a result, within a few months McClellan had an effectively organized, equipped, and drilled army.

On to Richmond! By the end of 1861 McClellan commanded 185,000 men, at the time the largest army ever assembled in America. What the Union general intended to do with his mag-

The Trans-Mississippi Theater

nificent Army of the Potomac remained unclear. Most Northerners thought he ought to move it into Virginia and immediately engage the enemy. "On to Richmond!" was again heard. But McClellan seemed in no hurry. A superb drillmaster, he improved his army each day. Besides, it was much easier to cry "On to Richmond!" than it was to get there. Geography was strongly against the advance of troops across the country between Washington and the Confederate capital. The numerous parallel rivers that intersected the Virginia coastal plain between the Blue Ridge Mountains and Chesapeake Bay lay directly across the path of the invader, creating obstructions for northern armies marching overland on Richmond, and providing Confederates excellent defensive positions. McClellan, thinking more about saving his men from defeat and not enough, perhaps, about leading them to victory, held his fine army in check. Summer passed, autumn passed, the year 1861 passed, and still he made no advance on Richmond.

The Invasion of New Mexico. While the Federals hesitated, the Confederates acted. In February 1862 Confederate Gen. Henry H. Sibley led 2,500 Texan cavalrymen into New Mexico Territory, hoping to seize the entire Southwest for the Confederacy. He outflanked Federal Gen. Edward R.S. Canby's 2,800 regulars and New Mexico Volunteers at the fierce Battle of Val Verde on February 21, and then captured Albuquerque and Santa Fe. But on March 28 the Confederates suffered a strategic defeat at Glorieta Pass, after Col. Manuel Chavez discovered Sibley's supply train, which the Federals destroyed. Outnumbered and starving, the Texans retreated to El Paso, Texas. Thus ended a disastrous adventure and Confederate hopes of controlling the Southwest. Sibley lost over a third of his men; Federal casualties numbered only about 350.

Chapter Six

BEHIND THE LINES

Foreign Complications. The establishment of the Confederacy created serious international problems for Lincoln's government. A chief cause of friction with foreign powers was the blockade that the President declared immediately after the fall of Fort Sumter. The purpose of the blockade was to prevent the South from selling its cotton and other staples to the countries of Europe and receiving in exchange not only guns, ammunition, and various military supplies, but also clothing, shoes, medicines, and other articles of daily use. Northerners reasoned that the South would be severely handicapped if it were deprived of foreign trade, for it had few industries. The Confederacy was never completely cut off—there was always some blockade running—yet normal trade with Europe ceased even before the fighting began, and in less than a year the coast was so well guarded that only the swiftest and boldest craft risked the danger of running the blockade.

The Blockade and International Relations. Considered as a war measure, the blockade was of incalculable value to the North, for it struck the South at its weakest point. But since striking this blow at the same time inflicted injuries upon the trade of foreign nations it was bound to have an unfortunate effect upon Federal international relations. Lincoln wanted to treat secession as a family quarrel from which outsiders should

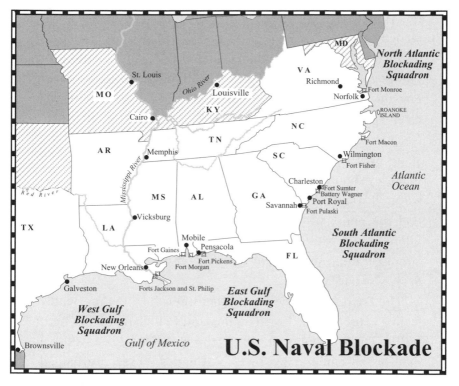

stand clear. He did not want to regard the disturbance as a war but as a mere uprising that he could suppress with the militia. Congress at no time declared war against the Confederacy, but on May 6, 1861, the Confederate Congress passed an act recognizing the existence of war between the United States and the Confederate States. When Lincoln made the call for troops he did so by virtue of a law passed in 1795 giving the President the power to use the militia in suppressing insurrections. It was his theory that on land the Confederate troops were insurgents and that on sea Confederate vessels were engaged in piracy. But when he announced the blockade he virtually admitted that he was waging a war with the South, for in the eyes of international law a blockade assumes the existence of belligerency. Taking this view, Great Britain, as soon as the blockade was declared, recognized the Confederate States as belligerents and proclaimed itself a neutral nation. Most of the leading nations of Europe followed the British example. In the North the action of England in recognizing the Confederacy as a belligerent was resented as evidence of unfriendliness toward the United States. Great Britain's acknowledgment gave Confederate cruisers the status of privateers, while it was the policy and desire of Lincoln that they should be regarded as pirates. England, however, was within its rights and justified in the course it took. It happened that the policy of neutrality was in line with England's own interests and with those of the Confederacy, and helped the South get more supplies for carrying on the war than it might otherwise have obtained.

The Trent Affair. The *Trent* Affair intensified the unfriendly feeling caused in the North by England's proclamation of neutrality. On November 8, 1861, the *San Jacinto*, a Federal man-of-war commanded by Capt. Charles Wilkes, overhauled the British mail steamship *Trent* and forcibly removed James M. Mason and John Slidell, Confederate commissioners enroute to England and France, who were taken to Boston and imprisoned. The *Trent* was then allowed to proceed to its destination. The incident delighted Northerners, and Wilkes became a popular hero. The House of Representatives thanked him and the secretary of the navy wrote him a note of congratulation. Even Secretary Seward was pleased at first. But officials of the Lincoln government were sobered when the English authorities demanded the release of Mason and Slidell. Seward, even before he heard from England, came to the conclusion that it was best to disclaim authority for the arrest. Great Britain, in demanding the release of the commissioners, pointed out that as a neutral state it was upholding the same principles that the United States had always strongly favored—namely that a neutral vessel should not be subjected to the right of search. After taking into consideration all the circumstances of the seizure, Seward decided that the captives must be given up: "We are asked to do to the British nation just what we have always insisted all nations ought to do to us." Mason and Slidell were released, placed on an English vessel, and made their way to Europe.

King Cotton Diplomacy. As reluctant as the Federals were to release the Confederate commissioners, they wanted no breach with England. Relations between the North and England were already strained, and indeed, Russia seemed to be the only European friend of the United States. Federal officials feared that if they refused to release Mason and Slidell, England might recognize Confederate independence. They knew that the South's cotton, now prevented by the blockade from reaching Europe, was important to England as well as to France and Belgium. The cotton textile industry employed a fourth of England's population: one-tenth of its wealth was invested in the industry, and cotton goods made up nearly half of England's export trade. Many Southerners believed that England must have the South's cotton to survive; consequently, if deprived of that cotton, Britain would intervene in the war on the side of the South.

"King Cotton Diplomacy" rested on this belief that England would be forced to recognize the Confederacy's independence. But England failed to act as Southerners expected, because in 1861 English warehouses were stuffed with a two-year surplus of raw cotton and finished cotton goods. The British cotton textile industry faced bankruptcy. Production had slowed, and British financial and economic writers predicted a long period of unemployment and suffering for textile workers. But the Civil War, by cutting off the supply of cheap cotton from America, was an answer to British problems. During the war the price of raw cotton rose from fourteen to sixty cents a pound, and the surplus British manufactured goods sold at a profit of more than $200,000,000. Being deprived of the South's cotton saved European textile manufacturers from one of the worst panics in history. No wonder members of the British Parliament from the industrial areas sat silently during the debates on intervention in the American Civil War.

Propaganda. Propaganda may have had less effect on diplomatic affairs than cotton surplus profits, yet both the North and the South used their own versions of the truth to influence Europeans. Early in the war the able and talented William L. Yancey represented the Confederacy in Europe, pleading its cause and promising "cotton and free trade, treaties on the most favorable footing—if only independence were favored." To offset this appeal Seward not only appointed the best men he could find to the diplomatic posts but also sent abroad private citizens of experience and ability—such as Thurlow Weed, the veteran journalist and politician—who tried to influence politicians and the local press and to win sympathy for the Union cause.

Intrusion into Mexico. Neither diplomacy nor propaganda prevented Napoleon III from using the war to promote the glory of France. He planted French power in the western hemisphere while Federals and Confederates struggled against each other. In 1861 Napoleon induced England and Spain to join France in sending armed forces into Mexico to collect the claims of their citizens against the government of that republic. England and Spain, convinced that Napoleon had ulterior designs, soon withdrew their forces, leaving France to act alone. Napoleon went on with his plans and, having overthrown the existing Mexican government, placed Maximilian, a brother of the Austrian emperor, on a throne supported by French troops. All this, of course, violated the Monroe Doctrine, but protests by the United States went unheeded until after the war.

English Conduct. The conduct of France in Mexico, although irritating and embarrassing, was by no means so disquieting to the Lincoln government as the conduct of England. Britain provided shelter in colonial ports for Confederate cruisers. Blockade running was almost exclusively a British and a Confederate activity. British agents served as Confederate agents and emissaries; British capitalists invested in Confederate bonds; and British merchants sold ammunition and weapons to the Confederate army. But, most irritating to Northerners, England permitted Confederate naval vessels to be constructed in English shipyards. The war had hardly begun before the keel of the cruiser *Florida* was laid, and by August 1, 1861, the contract was signed for the building of the *Alabama.*

Confederate Raiders. These vessels, built for the purpose of preying on Federal shipping, were allowed to leave British ports, and by the time the war was well under way they were out on the ocean. Confederate raiders destroyed 257 ships and forced Union ship owners to transfer over 700 American vessels to foreign registries. The United States merchant marine failed to recover from such destructiveness for over half a century.

Resources Compared. In 1860 the areas that supported the Federal government could claim over 22,000,000 people compared to the Confederacy's 9,000,000, only 5,500,000 of whom were white. The inhabitants of New York and Pennsylvania alone outnumbered the white population of the Confederacy by over a million. More than eighty percent of the military-age white population lived in the states and territories that remained loyal to the Federal government. While the South strained to fill its armies, the North used only a relatively small part of its potential manpower—1,000,000 Southerners compared to 1,500,000 Northerners served three years or more in the army. The Federals enjoyed much greater industrial and financial superiority over the South. The North had 110,000 manufacturing establishments producing $1,500,000,000 worth of goods compared to the South's 20,000 establishments producing $155,000,000 worth of goods. The manufacturing of all eleven Confederate states equaled in value only slightly more than fifty per cent of the manufacturing of Massachusetts alone. In 1860 the Union boasted 21,000 miles of railroad compared to the Confederacy's 9,000 miles, and that year the South produced only nineteen of the 470 locomotives made in America.

Financing the War. Both sides suffered from inflation during the war. To help stabilize finances, the North established a National Banking System in 1863 that required national banks to have one third of their capital invested in United States securities and authorized them to issue notes up to ninety percent of such bond holdings. The Confederates—handicapped by the inability to raise substantial loans, inadequate banking facilities, and opposition to taxation—faced a disastrous economic situation. Loans provided over $115,000,000 and taxation a similar sum, including a ten percent tax "in kind" on agricultural produce. The Confederates issued over a billion dollars in paper notes, which depreciated to thirty-three cents in gold by 1863 and to less than two cents by 1865. The Union's paper money, called "greenbacks," dropped to a low of thirty-nine cents in 1864.

The Northern Home Front. The war increased the North's prosperity. Wages lagged, but production, prices, and profits soared. Between 1860 and 1865 wages rose forty-three percent, while prices rose 117 percent. A continuous flow of immigrants—almost 800,000 during the war—and the adoption of labor-saving devices by industry and agriculture compensated for the loss of manpower to the army. Adoption of the Homestead Act in 1862 encouraged westward agricultural expansion.

Bumper crops met not only the increased home demand but also that from abroad. Great Britain acquired little cotton from the South but abundant wheat from the North.

Life Behind the Lines in the South. The South raised sufficient food to supply its people. Women supervised farms once directed by their husbands who were now in the army. By 1863, however, the breakdown of southern railroads brought hardship and near starvation to some areas. Moreover, the war ultimately crippled southern agriculture. Cotton production dropped with the dislocation of foreign markets from 4,500,000 bales in 1861 to 299,000 bales in 1864.

Not only did cotton production decline during the war, but so did every other agricultural activity. Livestock production fell everywhere in the South, but in some states more than in others. In South Carolina, for example, the hog population declined from 965,000 in 1860 to fewer than 150,000 in 1865. In describing the "devastation" of South Carolina by the Federals, one observer noted that "the larger portion of the Country [has been] utterly stript of its Stock." In 1860, the South raised two-thirds of the nation's swine—by 1880 it raised less than half. Eight of the former slave states produced some 2,600,000 fewer hogs in 1880 than they had in 1860. The war and its aftermath destroyed the southern tradition of grazing livestock on the open range.

Other activities suffered as well. Rice production declined to only forty percent of what it had been in 1861, and sugar production fell by more than fifty percent. The destructiveness of Union and Confederate armies accounted for some of these losses because foraging soldiers stole what livestock they encountered. The men either ate the animals or drove them away. Besides stealing livestock, they frequently burned fence rails and destroyed farm equipment. Confederate agriculturists also suffered from the depreciation of Confederate currency and securities, the Federal wartime confiscatory policies, and the instability of the southern labor supply.

Women of the 1860s. The Civil War affected the women of the 1860s in various ways. Nearly all females—old and young, rich and poor, black and white, slave and free, Confederate and Unionist—became involved. Some, because of family relationships or where they lived, remained relatively isolated from the conflict, but most suffered varying degrees of stress, and many experienced direct involvement in the horrors of war. The finest and the worst traits of "American womanhood" came to the surface during the war. All areas and each side had a number of selfless, dedicated, energetic, courageous, and virtuous women as well as those who were selfish, indifferent, cowardly, lazy, and immoral. Most northern and southern women idealized their respective causes and gave intense devotion and strenuous labor to support the war effort.

Active Service. Throughout the conflict women on both sides served as nurses, couriers, scouts, spies, and even as soldiers. At least 3,200 women held paid positions as army nurses, North and South. Not one of them became a great organizer like Florence Nightingale, but the South remembered with pride Fannie Beers and Kate Cummings just as the North revered Mary Ann Bickerdyke and Clara Barton, who truthfully boasted that she "went in while the battle raged." Gen. Ulysses S. Grant ranked "Mother" Bickerdyke as one of the most heroic figures of the war. Into government offices in both capitals poured a cohort of earnest workers, those in Richmond even braver than the civil servants of Washington in their willingness to face scorn and defamation. Long before the war ended, northern women flocked south to teach the freedmen and many southern women turned, despite the deep prejudices of the section, to teaching and to business pursuits, and some of them were ready to give former slaves a helping hand.

During the war women assumed new roles that prepared them to become more active agents in American society after the war—writers, civil servants, and managers of estates and businesses. From the war's outset women displayed their patriotism by helping to provision troops and by urging their menfolk to join the army. Southern women especially made joining the army a prerequisite to social acceptance. One Confederate lady confessed to a friend, "I wouldn't even look at a nonresistant." As Union soldiers occupied southern territory, they found the local women more difficult to conquer than southern males.

Nor did women always remain behind the lines. Army camps often "teemed with women." Wives of officers, female camp employees—cooks and laundresses—and prostitutes frequently gave encampments a decidedly feminine air. A soldier reported, "a bevy of nyumphs disheveled and rumpled but as much at home as though they had campaigned all their lives. The hour was early and the women were preparing breakfast, their hair tousled and bodices unlaced, while the camp bore all the marks of femininity, with hoop skirts and abbreviated pantaloons hung on trees, and the baggage of officers mingled in admirable confusion with crumpled dimity and calico." More than 400 women passed as soldiers and played a full military role until discovered, often to the embarrassment of veterans. "One of my sergeants was just delivered of a bouncing baby boy, which is in violation of all military regulations," Gen. William S. Rosecrans complained.

Homefront Suffering. Many women experienced hardship at home. Especially in the South, women bore many of the burdens of disrupted and sometimes deplorable conditions behind the lines. Great was the courage of those who found it a heroic task, in all sections, just to keep themselves and their families alive during years of privation and trial. Females left in remote or invaded areas sometimes begged their soldier husbands to desert, but others displayed unselfish devotion. Phoebe Pemberton Yates nursed Confederate soldiers and protected the government's medicinal whiskey supply from them. Other women farmed alone until supplies ran out, demonstrating courage and skill. Kate Stone, like a number of other mothers, moved her children to Texas. Some refugees fled their homes and had to wander aimlessly for months or years, living in outbuildings, tents, caves, forests, and fields. To go or to stay, when Union soldiers threatened their homes, was an agonizing decision. As Federal forces advanced on Columbia, South Carolina, "trains pulled from the depot with human cargo jammed inside and hanging on the top. Yet thousands unable to get a place were left behind. Roads were congested with families hauling as much portable property as they could manage. As fires broke out in the city, additional thousands were rendered homeless." Such were the experiences of hundreds of thousands of women during the struggle—they would never forget. After the war a Confederate officer remarked in his diary that his son was being taught by southern women to hate Northerners: "The child's bread is buttered with hatred, his milk is sweetened with it, his top spins and his ball bounces with it." The ghosts and scars of the conflict frequently survived in the bitter memories and on the lips of southern women. Just as Ezekiel noted in the Old Testament: "parents got the sour grapes, but the children got the sour taste."

Chapter Seven
WAR FOR SOUTHERN INDEPENDENCE

From Insurrection to Civil War. After the first important engagement at Manassas the conflict expanded from an insurrection into a civil war. Northerners, willing to conquer the South to save the Union, offered no compromises. Southerners, fighting to preserve their independence and to protect their homes and families, were just as willing to die for their cause. Thus began America's most momentous struggle. The outcome would change the nation's destiny.

Southern Disadvantages. The North's tremendous advantages over the South in manpower and resources gave the Federals a significant edge. The North—with twenty-two states against the South's eleven—had a potential military population of nearly 5,000,000. The South, on the other hand, strained to muster 1,000,000 men. The advantages in wealth and resources were all with the North. The South, for example, had made little progress in the manufacture of iron, an indispensable article of war. To obtain weapons, the Confederacy would have to make their own, capture arms from the Federals, or purchase guns abroad. The North's superior railroads made it possible for the

Federals to mobilize troops quickly and to place them at strategic points as well as to keep trade open between the East and the West, even if the South kept the Mississippi River closed to Union commerce.

Soldiers Compared. The soldiers were as different as the people of the regions. "Southern soldiers have éélan, courage, woodcraft, consummate horsemanship, endurance to pain equal to the Indians," observed Union Gen. Winfield Scott, a native Southerner, "but they will not submit to discipline. They will not take care of things or husband their resources. If it could be done by one wild desperate dash they would do it, but they cannot stand the waiting. . . . Men of the North on the other hand can wait; they can bear discipline; they can endure forever. Losses in battles were nothing to them. They will fight to the bitter end."

A Southern Advantage. In most things the North had an overwhelming advantage, but in one important respect the outlook favored the South. The North wanted to save the Union, to maintain the integrity of the nation. To do this it would have to be the aggressor, the invader. It would have to fight an offensive war—it would have to conquer and crush a country five times as large as France. The South, desiring only to be let alone, need not go out and conquer—all it had to do was to defend itself against the invader. It could maintain its independence without conquering a single foot of northern territory.

The Economy of Defense. There were excellent reasons then for the South to remain on the defensive. Offensive operations almost certainly would exhaust the Confederacy more quickly than the Union because invasions and tactical offensives used up more men and resources than defenses. As a rule, defense was the most economical form of warfare. Civil War defenders enjoyed even greater advantages than usual because tactics lagged behind military technology. The rifled musket, which replaced the smoothbore muzzleloader as the standard infantry weapon in the 1860s, gave the defense at least three times the strength of the offense. It would have been possible—at least theoretically—for the Confederates, using defensive tactics, to have remained in their entrenchments and to have destroyed the federal army, which had only a three-to-two manpower advantage over the Confederates, before the South exhausted its own human resources.

Davis Decides to Attack. At the conflict's outset President Jefferson Davis announced that the Confederacy was "waging this war solely for self-defense," thus implying that the South would concentrate on warding off Federal attacks. But his statement was more propaganda than actual intent. Davis preferred offensive to defensive warfare and so did most Confederates.

From the war's beginning southern sentiment favored invading the North. Confederate Secretary of State Robert Toombs announced in May 1861 that he was for "taking the initiative, and carrying the war into the enemy's country." He opposed any delay. "We must invade or be invaded," he contended. John B. Jones, a clerk in the Confederate war office, feared that the government's military policy might be defensive. If so, he warned, "it will be severely criticized, for a vast majority of our people are for carrying the war . . . [into the North] without a moment's delay." After the Battle of Manassas, President Davis indicated that he favored taking the offensive. "Never heard I more hearty cheering," Jones wrote in his diary. "Every one believed our banners would wave in the streets of Washington in a few days. The President had pledged himself . . . to carry the war into the enemy's country. . . . Now the people were well pleased with their President." Davis called his policy defensive-offensive strategy, but in reality, it was offensive warfare.

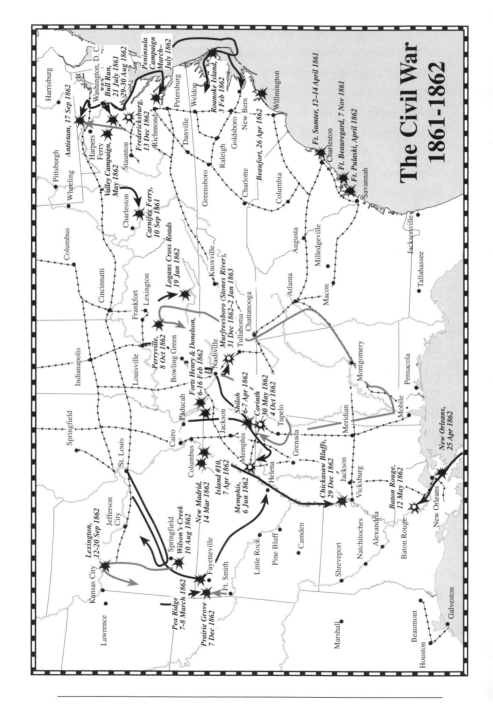

The Civil War
1861-1862

The Confederate Goal. The Confederates took the tactical offensive more often than their opponents early in the war in hopes of winning a quick victory before they exhausted their manpower and resources. They believed that if they could crush or capture one or more large Federal armies the Lincoln government might consider conquering the South too expensive.

The Confederates failed to achieve this goal. They attacked in eight of the first twelve big battles of the war, and in these eight assaults 97,000 Confederates fell—20,000 more men than the Federals lost in these same battles. Thus, in the first three years of the war, the South almost bled itself to death by taking the tactical offensive in nearly seventy percent of the major battles. "There is an insane desire on the part of the Southern people, & some of the Generals to assume the offensive," observed an officer in 1864. "Our successes have consisted in driving back the enemy & in defeating their attempt to invade. Our failures [result from our] . . . attempts to carry the war into their territory."

Forced to Become Defensive. After 1863 the Confederates attacked less often. Unsuccessful offensives had used up too much of the South's limited manpower, and forced the Confederacy to a defensive strategy.

They remained on the defensive in seven of the last ten major campaigns of the war, but in these actions Confederate forces frequently met enemy advances with counterattacks. Confederate generals would have attacked more frequently if their forces could have been replenished, but as the war drained Confederate manpower, the Federals compounded the South's problem by refusing to exchange prisoners. "If we commence a system of exchange which liberates all prisoners taken," observed Gen. Ulysses S. Grant, "we will have to fight on until the whole South is exterminated."

High Cost of Offensives. Casualty lists reveal that the Confederates destroyed themselves by making bold and repeated attacks. Confederate generals ordered tactical offensives in ninety-one percent of the battles in which they suffered their greatest percentage losses. In contrast, Confederate forces defended in eighty-nine percent of the battles in which they suffered the lowest percentage of casualties. Throughout the war the side that attacked usually suffered the most casualties, both proportionally and often absolutely. In only four battles (Cedar Mountain, Port Hudson, Fort Wagner, and Kennesaw Mountain)—each a relatively minor affair—were the Confederates able to inflict upon the Federals casualties that exceeded by ten percent or more those suffered by the Confederates themselves. Although the Federals attacked and suffered heavy casualties in these four battles, few were sustained assaults against strong positions. When Union attacks failed the generals usually learned not to try such tactics again. To have suffered in four years of combat only four relatively minor assaults in which their casualties exceeded their opponents' by ten percent or more is quite remarkable for an army that was forced by the political nature of the conflict to invade and conquer.

The Federals made plenty of blunders. Union forces were saved from making wasteful assaults because the Confederates were so willing to take the initiative.

Attack and Die. Throughout the war, bloody Confederate offensives took the lives of the bravest southern officers and men. In half of the twenty-two major battles or campaigns of the Civil War the Federals attacked, losing 119,000 men on assaults and 88,000 in defensive operations. The Confederates lost 117,000 men on attacks, but only 61,000 while defending. In other words, every time the Confederates attacked they lost an average of ten more men out of every hundred engaged than the

Federal defenders, but when the Confederates defended, they lost seven fewer men out of every hundred than the Union attackers. In the first dozen major campaigns, when the Confederates were more often the aggressor, every southern general sustained greater average percentage losses than his opponents. The Confederacy wasted not just its soldiers but its officers as well by attacking so often early in the war. Throughout the conflict Rebel generals attacked and died with their men. Fifty-five percent of all Confederate generals were killed or wounded in battle, and more generals—seventy percent—lost their lives leading attacks than any other way. A Northerner pointed out that "Southern leaders were . . . bolder in taking risks than their opponents, but also that they pushed their forces under fire very nearly to the limits of endurance." But risking their own and their men's lives in assault after assault brought them unbearable losses rather than decisive victories.

Gathering Armies. Neither side was prepared for war, but by the end of 1861 both the North and the South had assembled sizable armies. At the beginning of 1862 Union military forces consisted of nearly 500,000 men and the Union navy numbered more than 200 armed vessels. The Confederates had gathered together maybe half as many men and considerably fewer naval vessels. Most of the Federal troops were concentrated near Washington in the East and between St. Louis and Louisville in the West. The main Confederate concentrations were in Virginia and along a thin defense line across the Tennessee mountains to the Mississippi. Southerners also stationed troops at points along the Mississippi River and on the Gulf and Atlantic coasts.

Federal Plans. Lincoln wanted to invade and conquer the South. He and his advisers decided that to win the Federals must do four things: capture Richmond; maintain a naval

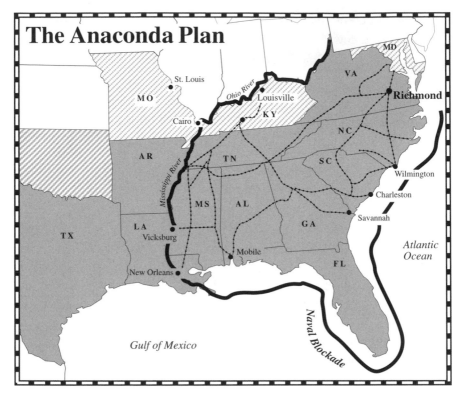

The Anaconda Plan

blockade of the South; gain control of the Mississippi River, which would cut the Confederacy into two parts and give the North an outlet to the sea; and press southward until every foot of the Confederacy was brought under Federal control. This meant pressure in Virginia, and along the coast. But first of all, the North needed to take action in the West.

Chapter Eight

WAR IN THE WEST IN 1862

Importance of the West. Federal Gen. William T. Sherman predicted correctly that the Civil War would be won in the West, where the initial campaigns of 1862 began, but neither he nor anyone else realized the effort needed for such a victory. It soon became clear that the western Confederacy would be difficult to defend: its long coastline was vulnerable to attack at various points; its few rail lines compounded the problem of shifting Confederate troops about to threatened points; and its waterways, which generally ran north and south, invited invasion. The Federals, enjoying naval superiority, had the opportunity to attack the coastal towns and penetrate deep into the Southwest with their gunboats. They eventually managed to split the Confederacy by capturing the Mississippi River and then driving the Confederate armies eastward to final defeat. But all this took time and the lives of many soldiers.

Ulysses S. Grant. The man who was foremost in directing Federal movements in the West was Ulysses Simpson Grant. At the war's outbreak he was thirty-nine years old and considered a failure. Trained for war at the United States Military Academy, he was proficient in mathematics and the best horseman in his class. During the Mexican War he had served in both Taylor's and Scott's armies, participated in most of the important action, and won distinction for personal gallantry. But in 1854, after a drinking problem got him in trouble, he resigned from the army and settled near St. Louis, where he failed at farming and at selling real estate. He then moved with his family to Galena, Illinois, a broken and disappointed man, to work in his father's store for $800 a year until the war began.

In June 1861, he secured an appointment as colonel of an Illinois regiment and in August he became a brigadier general of volunteers. Grant would move upward from one position to another until he became the central military figure of the war. Round-shouldered, short, and not at all striking in personal appearance, he "has rough, light-brown whiskers, blue eyes, and a rather scrubbly look withal," noted an observer. "But his face is firm and hard and his eye is clear and resolute." On the battlefield his physical courage seemed remarkable even to brave men. Through rattling musketry fire, with bullets flying all around, Grant would sit quietly and imperturbably in his saddle. Direct in manner and persevering in action, he was as straightforward in his tactics as in his personal relations, hammering away until he won. Like most able generals, Grant enjoyed combat.

Fort Henry and Fort Donelson. He struck the first effective blow delivered by the Union army when he attacked Fort Henry on the Tennessee River and Fort Donelson on the Cumberland. These were very important Confederate positions, guarding waterways that led far into the center of the Confederacy. On February 6, 1862, in cooperation with a flotilla of gunboats commanded by Commodore Andrew H. Foote, Grant captured Fort Henry, and then marched overland with 27,000 men against Fort Donelson, which surrendered on February 16. His victory—which cost in casualties 2,800 Federals and 17,000 Confederates (including

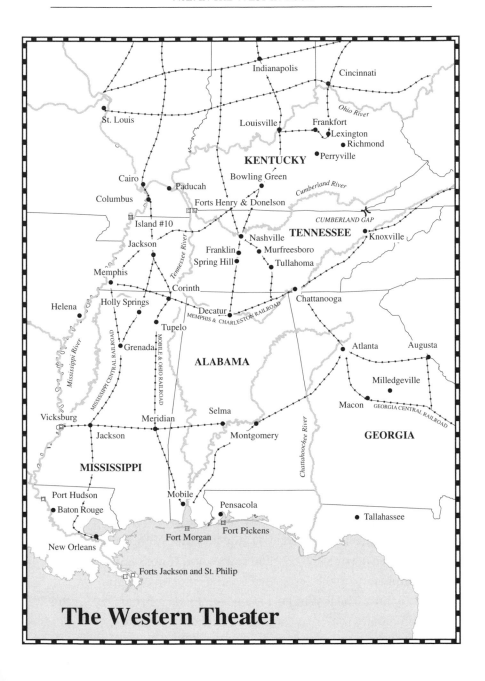

The Western Theater

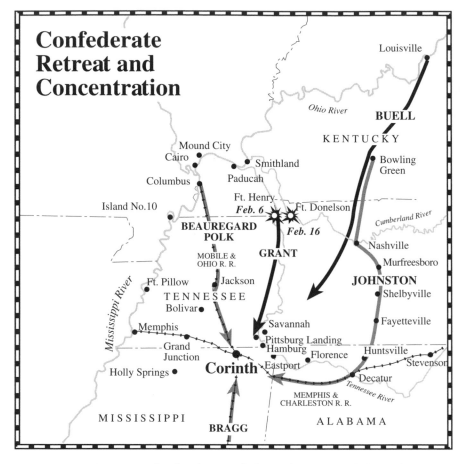

Confederate Retreat and Concentration

15,000 prisoners)—broke the Confederacy's western defense line, brought the whole of Kentucky and much of Tennessee under Federal control, and opened a route into the South. The capital of Tennessee fell quickly to Union troops and Grant's army steamed triumphantly up the Tennessee River toward Mississippi.

Corinth. The loss of Fort Donelson made it necessary for the Confederates to retreat southward to Corinth, an important railroad junction in northeastern Mississippi. There Gen. Albert Sydney Johnston, whom President Davis considered his best general, rallied and reorganized an army of 40,000 men. Meanwhile, Grant had disembarked his 41,000 men at Pittsburg Landing, near Shiloh Church, just across the Tennessee line from Corinth, to await the arrival of Gen. Don Carlos Buell's 30,000 reinforcements marching from Nashville.

Shiloh. Johnston decided that he must attack and destroy Grant before Buell joined him; otherwise, the united Federals would be too strong to oppose. On April 6, to Grant's surprise, Johnston's men attacked at Shiloh before Buell's men arrived. All day the Confederates surged forward and in fierce fighting forced the Federals back to the river. In this bloody action, General Johnston was killed. Command passed to Gen. Pierre Gustave Toutant Beauregard, who ended the action before dark, believing Grant to be whipped. During the night Buell arrived with fresh troops and the next morning Grant counterattacked. The Confederates, now outnumbered and facing fresh troops, fell back to Corinth. The Federals were too exhausted to follow. During the two days of action nearly 14,000 Federals and 11,000 Confederates were killed, wounded, or captured—at the time the heaviest casualties ever suffered in battle by Americans.

More Confederate Disasters. Other Confederate disasters followed. Within two months after Shiloh the Federals had gained control of both ends of the Mississippi River. On April 25, New Orleans, the largest city and banking center of the South, surrendered to Commander David G. Farragut. On June 6, after a gunboat battle, Union forces took Memphis. The Confederates abandoned Corinth and retreated southward. By the summer of 1862 Confederates controlled only a small portion of the Mississippi River between Vicksburg, Mississippi, and Port Hudson, Louisiana—the middle of the Confederacy was being pinched from both ends.

The Kentucky Campaign. As both sides reorganized in Mississippi, the Confederates launched a two-pronged invasion of Kentucky led by Gen. Braxton Bragg, who had replaced the ailing

Beauregard, and by Gen. Edmund Kirby Smith. Outflanking General Buell, who had been moving eastward toward Chattanooga, Tennessee, the Confederates captured Lexington, Kentucky, and threatened Louisville and Cincinnati. Buell's army of 40,000 men, racing northward, confronted 16,000 of Bragg's men at Perryville, Kentucky, on October 8. After an indecisive action that cost each side about 3,000 casualties, Bragg withdrew from Kentucky because too few Kentuckians had joined his army and the reinforcements he had expected from Mississippi had been defeated on October 3 and 4 at Iuka and Corinth by Gen. William S. Rosecrans, who now replaced Buell.

Murfreesboro (Stones River). Bragg retreated to Murfreesboro, Tennessee, thirty miles southeast of Rosecrans's Nashville headquarters. Late in December, after 9,000 of Bragg's men had been sent to reinforce Vicksburg, Rosecrans moved south with 47,000 men. Bragg, commanding about 38,000 troops, impatiently attacked the Federals on December 31, 1862, and January 2, 1863, at Murfreesboro on Stones River, but failed to break their line. His unsuccessful assaults cost the Confederates nearly 12,000 casualties and the Union defenders nearly 13,000. Unable to drive back the Federal army, Bragg retreated southward. Rosecrans failed to pursue.

Mississippi. Late in 1862, Grant launched an abortive offensive against Vicksburg. He planned two attacks on the town: one by moving forces along the railroad from northern Mississippi to Jackson and then westward to Vicksburg, and a second by moving other forces down the Mississippi on a fleet of transports. The rail movement collapsed when Confederates destroyed the Federal supply depot in northern Mississippi. The water expedition failed when the Vicksburg fortifications proved too strong for an assault from the river. By January 1863, Grant's men were mired in the swamps north and west of Vicksburg.

Chapter Nine

WAR IN THE EAST IN 1862

The *Monitor* and the *Virginia*. Early in 1862, while Gen. George McClellan prepared for land action in the East, an important naval engagement occurred. On March 8 the Confederate ironclad *Virginia*, once a Federal vessel called the *Merrimac*, suddenly moved out from Norfolk, Virginia, and sank two of the wooden Union ships blockading the coast. The next day, it encountered the *Monitor*, a low-decked Federal ironclad with a revolving gun turret. Neither vessel won a decided victory but the *Virginia*, forced to retreat upriver and later scuttled, was prevented from doing further damage to the Union fleet. This naval duel in Hampton Roads marked the beginning of a new era in naval architecture. The day of the wooden warship was over; the picturesque domination by the oak-ribbed and white winged vessels had forever given way to steel and steam.

Up the Peninsula to Seven Pines. A few days after the battle between the ironclads, McClellan took his army by water from Washington to Fort Monroe, Virginia, from which he moved up the peninsula between the York and James rivers toward Richmond. He moved slowly, spending a month preparing to capture Yorktown, only to have the Confederates slip away just as he was about to attack. McClellan pursued and engaged them at

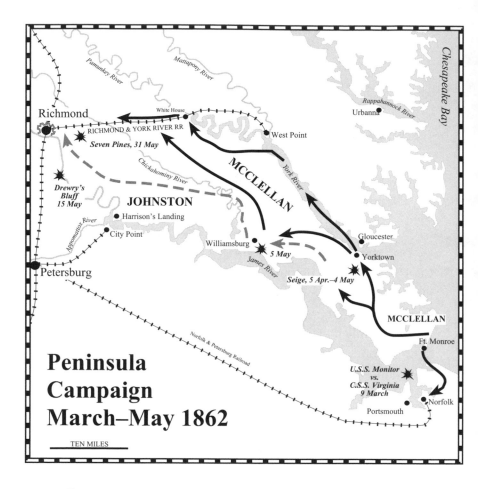

Peninsula Campaign March–May 1862

Williamsburg, but once again the Confederates withdrew toward Richmond. McClellan followed to within seven miles of the Confederate capital. There, at Seven Pines or Fair Oaks on May 31, Gen. Joseph E. Johnston's 42,000 Confederates attacked the 42,000 Federals caught astride the flooded Chickahominy River. In this battle McClellan suffered 4,000 casualties but repulsed the assault. Union soldiers inflicted 6,000 casualties on the Confederates. Johnston, wounded in the action, was replaced as army commander by Gen. Robert E. Lee.

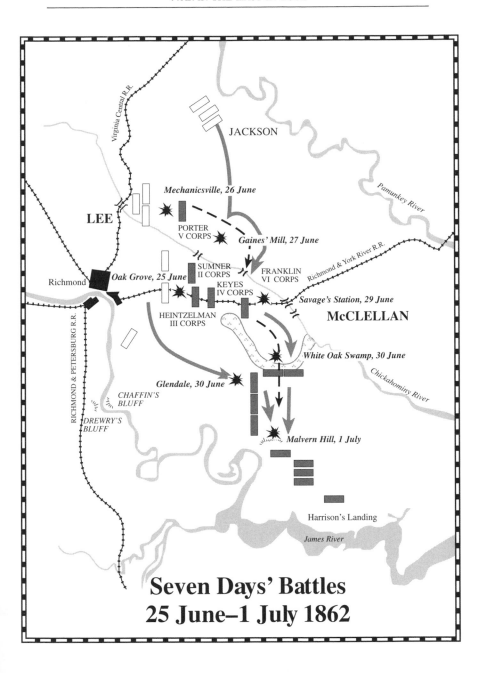

Seven Days' Battles
25 June–1 July 1862

Robert E. Lee. Lee would become the Confederacy's greatest general. Like many Confederate officers, he was in the U.S. Army at the war's outbreak, and was offered command of the Union army. Lee opposed slavery and secession, but when Virginia seceded he went with his state. He could not, he said, "raise my hand against my relatives, my children, my home." As a military leader, Lee was bold and daring. His military actions and courtly manner inspired his men and gave them confidence in their own courage and fighting ability. "General Lee was not given to indecision," reported the wife of President Davis, "and they have mistaken his character who supposed caution was his vice. He was prone to attack." Lee enjoyed combat as much as Grant.

The Seven Days. Lee intended to attack and destroy McClellan's army, which was waiting for reinforcements that Lincoln had held back to protect Washington. Since March, Confederate Gen. Thomas J. "Stonewall" Jackson, with only 16,000 men, had tied up 40,000 Union troops in the Shenandoah Valley. These were the troops McClellan wanted and expected. He never got them, but Lee got Jackson and his men. When Jackson's force arrived, the Seven Days' Battle began—95,000 Confederates against 92,000 Federals. Lee attacked on June 26 at Mechanicsville and the next day at Gaines's Mill. On June 29 the Confederate army assulted Savage Station and the next at Frayser's Farm or Glendale. Finally on July 1 Lee ordered an attach on Malvern Hill. Lee's assault drove McClellan back across the peninsula to a new base on the James River, but failed to destroy his army. Lee's fierce assaults cost the Confederates dearly—20,000 casualties, twice as many as the Federals suffered. But Richmond was saved.

Second Manassas (Second Bull Run). Lincoln, who never got along with McClellan, decided to make some changes. He

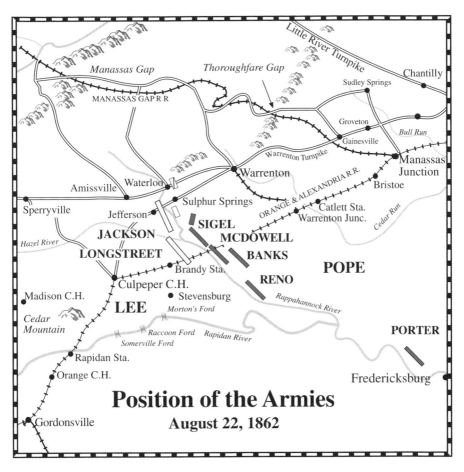

Position of the Armies
August 22, 1862

withdrew McClellan's men from the peninsula and appointed Gen. John Pope to command a new eastern field army. Pope, advancing boldly, encountered part of Lee's army—Stonewall Jackson's command—near the old Manassas or Bull Run battle-field in northeastern Virginia. On August 29 he attacked, but failed to dislodge Jackson. The next day Lee arrived with the other half of his army, attacked Pope's exposed flank, and routed the Union army. Casualties numbered 10,000 of the 76,000 Federals engaged, and 9,000 of the 49,000 Confederates engaged.

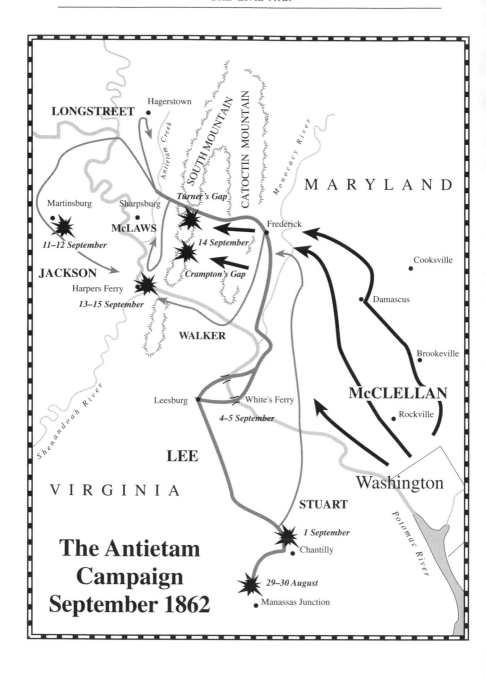

LONGSTREET

Hagerstown

SOUTH MOUNTAIN

CATOCTIN MOUNTAIN

Antietam Creek

Monocacy River

Turner's Gap

MARYLAND

Martinsburg

Sharpsburg

McLAWS

Frederick

14 September

Cooksville

11–12 September

Crampton's Gap

JACKSON

Harpers Ferry

Damascus

13–15 September

WALKER

Brookeville

McCLELLAN

Shenandoah River

Leesburg

White's Ferry

Rockville

4–5 September

LEE

VIRGINIA

Washington

STUART

Potomac River

1 September

**The Antietam
Campaign
September 1862**

Chantilly

29–30 August

Manassas Junction

Sharpsburg (Antietam). After Pope's disastrous defeat, Lincoln restored McClellan to command and sent him in pursuit of Lee, who had crossed the Potomac and marched into Maryland, where he expected to gain men and supplies. Lee also hoped that an invasion of the North would bring European recognition of the Confederacy and aid from abroad. After learning the location of Lee's divided army from a captured order, McClellan marched west and confronted at Sharpsburg, Maryland, part of Lee's command which was strung out along Antietam Creek and backed against the Potomac River. For a time McClellan believed he faced 120,000 men, but Lee never had more than 39,000 men on the battlefield. McClellan's delays allowed most of Jackson's Corps, which had been sent to capture the Federal garrison at Harpers Ferry, to rejoin Lee, but some of his troops had not yet arrived when the Federals attacked at Sharpsburg. The day of the assault, September 17, became the bloodiest single day of the war. Forced back by the Federal onslaught, the Confederates counterattacked and stubbornly maintained their position. Near the end of the day Gen. A.P. Hill's Light Division arrived after a forced march from Harpers Ferry and prevented Lee's right flank from being turned. Losses on both sides—12,000 men each—were enormous. Lee, after this narrow escape, retired across the Potomac. McClellan failed to press his advantage.

Fredericksburg. Lincoln then made a serious mistake. On November 7 he relieved McClellan from command and replaced him with Gen. Ambrose Burnside, who was a loyal subordinate but incapable of commanding an army. He lacked confidence in himself, and he inspired no confidence in his soldiers. In hopes of skirting Lee's right flank and getting between the Confederates and Richmond, he crossed the Rappahannock River at Fredericksburg where Lee was waiting for him with a line of troops. On

December 13, Burnside's 100,000 men advanced against Lee's well placed 72,000. The Federals were slaughtered, suffering 11,000 casualties to the Confederates' 5,000.

The Results of 1862. The Federals made some important gains in 1862. They failed to take Richmond, but made significant progress toward opening the Mississippi. Furthermore, they strengthened their naval blockade, and drove the Confederates out of western Virginia, Kentucky, Missouri, most of Tennesssee, half of Arkansas, and portions of Mississippi and Louisiana. In battles won and lost, Union armies had done better in the West and Confederate armies better in the East. Casualties on both sides had been staggering. The Confederates, who had lost more men than they could afford to lose, still hoped that their reckless assaults would gain them a decisive victory.

Emancipation. The Federal victory at Sharpsburg or Antietam gave Lincoln an opportunity to issue the Emancipation Proclamation. The President had no authority under the Constitution or under any law to emancipate a single slave, but as the war progressed Lincoln became determined to use freedmen in the Union war effort. The Confederates were already using slaves to produce food and staples, drive wagons, and dig entrenchments for the army. In 1861, the Federal Congress had passed a bill confiscating slaves "whose labor was used for insurrectionary purposes."

Lincoln signed the bill with great reluctance, for he feared the slave states that had remained in the Union would react unfavorably to such legislation. The President hoped that loyal slave owners would voluntarily emancipate their slaves and that freed blacks would be colonized outside the United States. In April 1862, Congress appropriated $1,000,000 to compensate slave owners and $100,000 to assist in colonization. Another antislavery law, the Confiscation Act, freed any slaves who crossed Federal lines or were captured in Confederate territory. The law also authorized the use of black troops, and allowed the President "to employ as many persons of African descent as may seem necessary and proper for the suppression of the rebellion."

Emancipation as a Military Necessity. Despite his desire to keep within constitutional limits, Lincoln realized that sentiment favoring emancipation was growing in the North. Some radical members of Congress urged the President, who soon reached the conclusion that emancipation was a military necessity. On September 23, five days after Sharpsburg, Lincoln issued a preliminary proclamation declaring that on January 1, 1863, "all persons held as slaves within any State or designated part of a State, the people whereof shall then be in rebellion against the United States, shall be then, thenceforward and forever free." Stripped of its propaganda, his proclamation freed no slaves; indeed, it declared free only those slaves under Confederate control and thus beyond Lincoln's authority. The proclamation left all blacks owned by loyal masters—those in territory controlled by the Federals—as enslaved as they had ever been.

Official Duty. The President explained what he was trying to accomplish in a letter to a critic. "My paramount purpose in this struggle is to save the Union, and is not either to save or destroy slavery," wrote Lincoln. "If I could save the Union without freeing any slave, I would do it; and if I could save it by freeing all the slaves I would do it; and if I could save it by freeing some and leaving others alone, I would also do that. What I do about slavery and the colored race I do because I believe it helps to save the Union; and what I forbear, I forbear because I do not believe it would help to save the Union. I shall do less whenever I shall believe what I am doing hurts the cause; and I shall do more whenever I shall believe doing more will help the cause. I shall try to correct errors when shown to be errors, and I shall adopt new views so fast as they shall appear to be true views. I have here stated my purpose according to my view of official duty."

Reaction in the North. Antislavery radicals hailed the proclamation, but Lincoln detected a lukewarm attitude in the North's response. While admitting that "commendation in newspapers and by distinguished individuals is all a vain man could wish," he worried because "stocks have declined and troops come forward more slowly than ever. This, looked soberly in the face, is not very satisfactory." The fall elections were particularly discouraging; Lincoln's party lost in New York, Pennsylvania, Ohio, Indiana, Illinois, and Wisconsin. The Republicans barely maintained their majority in the House, and would have lost control had not the presence of Federal troops ensured solid Republican delegations from Maryland, Kentucky, and Missouri.

The elections indicated that the voters lacked confidence in the administration, but Lincoln held firm to his purpose. He had come to believe that slavery was at the bottom of all the trouble. "Without slavery the rebellion could never have existed," he told Congress in December 1862; "without slavery it could not continue."

Reaction Elsewhere. Among slaveholders the proclamation reinforced their argument that Lincoln was the abolitionist they contended him to be and that the war was merely a crusade against slavery. Southerners treated the proclamation as an empty vaunt that strengthened their determination to resist. On January 12, 1863, President Davis, in a message to Congress, declared that the proclamation "encouraged the slaves to a general assassination of their masters." No slaves rebelled, but a number ran away and some of those joined the Federal army.

Abroad, especially in England, the proclamation cleared up doubts about the war and created a better feeling toward the North.

Black Troops. In 1863, freedmen began to join the Union army. Col. Robert Gould Shaw, a socially and intellectually prominent Bostonian, commanded the first black regiment, the 54th Massachusetts. Though generally used for garrison duty, black troops exhibited marked courage in several actions. Shaw's regiment charged bravely and suffered severe losses at Fort Wagner, South Carolina, in 1863. Confederates threatened to kill any white officer who commanded black units, but none was executed. Whether some Confederate soldiers deliberately killed rather than captured black soldiers is still disputed. Federals claimed that in April 1864 at Fort Pillow, on the Mississippi River north of Memphis, Gen. Nathan B. Forrest's troops massacred black troops who had surrendered. When demanding the surrender of the fort, Forrest had offered to accept the black soldiers as prisoners of war. The Confederates, who stormed the fort after the Federal commander refused to acquiesce, captured only fifty-eight of the 262 blacks engaged in the action. Confederates refused to exchange black prisoners and tried to identify and return to servitude all the escaped slaves that they captured. Even so, by 1865 more than 183,000 freedmen had joined the Union army.

Black Confederate Soldiers. Late in the war, after bitterly debating the issue for months, the Confederates decided to use black soldiers as well, but only after General Lee and President Davis gave the measure their full support. On March 13, 1865, the Confederate Congress passed an act authorizing the enlistment of black men. Upon induction into the army these slaves would become free. On March 15 a Virginia newspaper noted the effort to recruit slaves into Confederate service, and on April 15 a Georgia paper announced: "Negroes are now being enlisted . . . for service in the Confederate army." But the Confederates had waited too long to use their only untapped source of manpower; six days before the announcement in the Georgia newspaper, Lee had surrendered.

Chapter Ten
WAR IN 1863

Pessimism in the North. The Confederates had suffered some serious defeats in 1862, but the Union's disaster in December at Fredericksburg discouraged many Northerners. The Rebels unquestionably were still dangerous. Veteran Confederate armies faced the Federals in Virginia, Tennessee, Mississippi, Arkansas, and Louisiana. If they could just hold on to what remained of the Confederacy and continue to inflict such casualties as the Federals had suffered at Fredericksburg the North might yet abandon its attempt to conquer the South.

Chancellorsville. In the spring of 1863 Federal Gen. Joseph ("Fighting Joe") Hooker, who replaced Burnside as commander of the Army of the Potomac, planned to flank Lee and outrun him to Richmond. Hooker split his forces, leaving Gen. John Sedgwick's troops to demonstrate against Fredericksburg, while he crossed the Rappahannock River northwest of Lee's left flank. To counter this movement, Lee left only a rear guard to hold off Sedgwick and wheeled his badly outnumbered army of 57,000 men around to attack Hooker, who soon lost his aggressiveness and entrenched his 97,000 men around the crossroads of Chancellorsville. Ignoring military precedent, Lee divided his army, threatened Hooker's left, and boldly sent Jackson's Corps to attack the Union right flank. Just before dark on May 2, Jackson surprised and drove the Federals back more than two miles. The

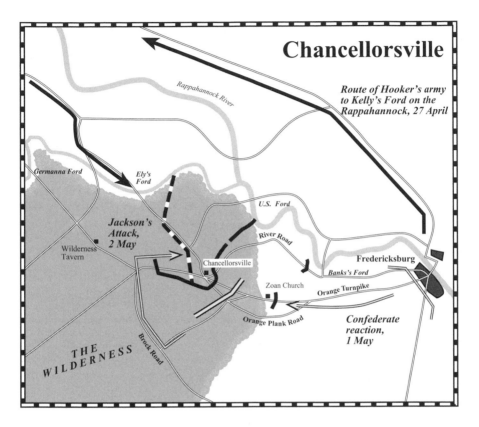

Chancellorsville

Route of Hooker's army
to Kelly's Ford on the
Rappahannock, 27 April

Rappahannock River

Germanna Ford

Ely's Ford

U.S. Ford

Jackson's Attack, 2 May

River Road

Wilderness Tavern

Chancellorsville

Fredericksburg

Banks's Ford

Zoan Church

Orange Turnpike

Confederate reaction, 1 May

Orange Plank Road

Brock Road

THE WILDERNESS

battle continued the next day, but on May 4 Hooker ended the action and withdrew his army across the river. At Fredericksburg, Sedgwick forced the Confederates back, but on May 4 he also retreated when Lee turned to attack him. Each side lost 11,000 men, but the Confederate casualties included Stonewall Jackson, who was fatally wounded.

Vicksburg. In the western theater in April 1863, after four unsuccessful attempts to capture Vicksburg, Mississippi, Grant began another effort. On the night of April 16, Commander David D. Porter successfully ran his ships past the Vicksburg batteries, thus making it possible for Grant to ferry his troops from Louisiana across the Mississippi River south of Vicksburg.

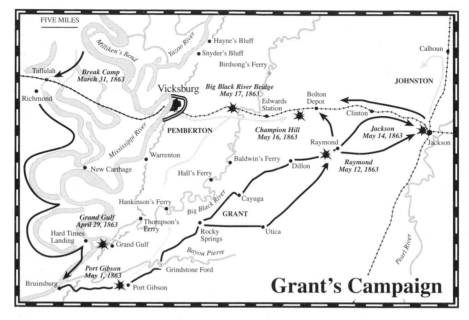

FIVE MILES

Hayne's Bluff
Snyder's Bluff
Birdsong's Ferry
Calhoun
JOHNSTON
Tallulah
Break Camp
March 31, 1863
Vicksburg
Big Black River Bridge
May 17, 1863
Bolton
Depot
Richmond
Edwards
Station
Clinton
PEMBERTON
Champion Hill
May 16, 1863
Jackson
May 14, 1863
Jackson
Warrenton
Raymond
New Carthage
Baldwin's Ferry
Dillon
Raymond
May 12, 1863
Hall's Ferry
Hankinson's Ferry
Cayuga
Grand Gulf
April 29, 1863
Thompson's
Ferry
GRANT
Hard Times
Landing
Grand Gulf
Rocky
Springs
Utica
Bayou Pierre
Port Gibson
May 1, 1863
Grindstone Ford
Bruinsburg
Port Gibson

Grant's Campaign

Striking inland, Grant moved east to Jackson, Mississippi and then turned back toward Vicksburg. Only then did Confederate Gen. John C. Pemberton venture out of his Vicksburg entrenchments to meet Grant. Two sharp engagements forced the Confederates back into the town. Grant then lost 3,000 men assaulting the strong Confederate defenses before besieging Vicksburg with his 45,000 men.

Confederate Gen. Joseph E. Johnston pulled together reinforcements from various garrisons but was still too weak to attack Grant. On July 4, after a siege of forty-two days, Pemberton surrendered the starving town and his 29,000 soldiers. Grant had won a major victory, which together with Gen. Nathaniel P. Banks's successful siege of Port Hudson, Louisiana, cut the Confederacy in two. The Federals had gained control of the entire Mississippi River.

Gettysburg. President Davis, although urged to send additional troops to Mississippi, decided instead to gamble that an

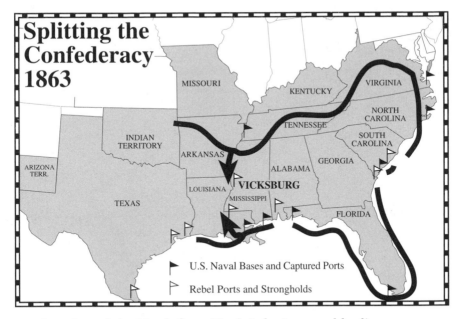

Splitting the Confederacy 1863

MISSOURI

KENTUCKY

VIRGINIA

NORTH CAROLINA

TENNESSEE

SOUTH CAROLINA

INDIAN TERRITORY

ARKANSAS

GEORGIA

ARIZONA TERR.

ALABAMA

LOUISIANA **VICKSBURG**

MISSISSIPPI

TEXAS

FLORIDA

▶ U.S. Naval Bases and Captured Ports

⌐ Rebel Ports and Strongholds

invasion of the North from Virginia by Lee would relieve pressure on Vicksburg. In June, Lee crossed the Potomac River heading for Pennsylvania. Gen. George G. Meade, who had replaced Hooker, moved north to meet Lee. Early in July the two armies clashed at Gettysburg, Pennsylvania. On July 1, as troops from both sides assembled, the Confederates drove the Federals back through the town to a strong defense position that resembled a fish hook. There Meade concentrated 83,000 men to face Lee's 75,000. Confederate attacks continued unsuccessfully for three days. On July 2 Confederate Gen. James Longstreet's men almost captured Little Round Top, a hill that dominated the left flank of the Union line. Finally, on July 3, having failed to break either Union flank, Lee sent 15,000 troops led by two heroic and romantic generals—Johnston Pettigrew and George Pickett—in a headlong charge against the Union center on Cemetery Ridge. Federal fire slaughtered the attackers and broke the assault. On July 4, the day Vicksburg surrendered, Lee evacuated his badly

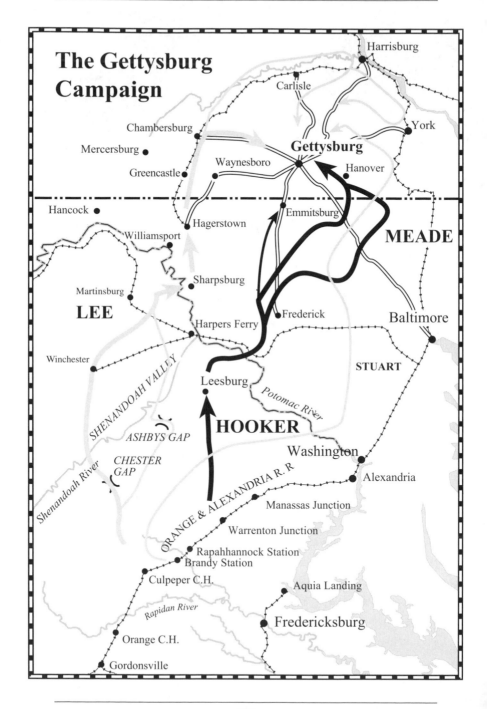

The Gettysburg Campaign

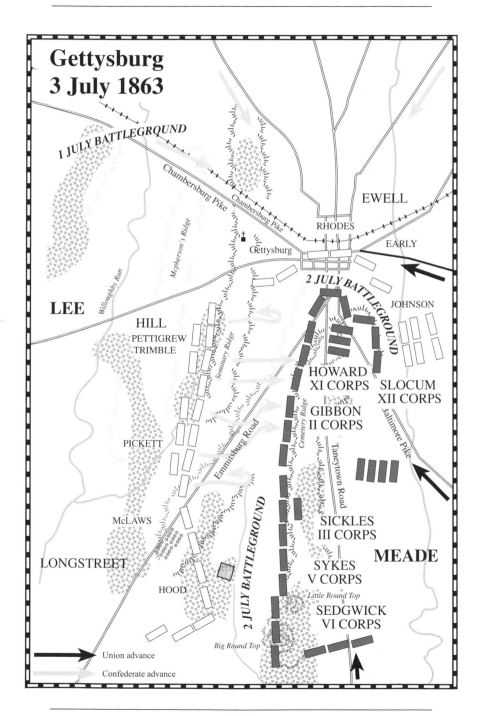

**Gettysburg
3 July 1863**

1 JULY BATTLEGROUND

Chambersburg Pike

Chambersburg Pike

EWELL

RHODES

EARLY

Willoughby Run

McpPherson's Ridge

Gettysburg

2 JULY BATTLEGROUND

JOHNSON

LEE

HILL
PETTIGREW
TRIMBLE

Seminary Ridge

HOWARD
XI CORPS

SLOCUM
XII CORPS

Baltimore Pike

PICKETT

Emmitsburg Road

Cemetery Ridge

GIBBON
II CORPS

Taneytown Road

McLAWS

SICKLES
III CORPS

MEADE

LONGSTREET

2 JULY BATTLEGROUND

SYKES
V CORPS

HOOD

Little Round Top

SEDGWICK
VI CORPS

Big Round Top

Union advance

Confederate advance

mauled army. Meade's battered Federals failed to pursue. Casualties were staggering—the Confederates lost 23,000 men, and the Union 18,000. The Battle of Gettysburg, because Lee lost so many men there, was a turning point in the war. From the summer of 1863 until the end of the war, Lee was compelled to be less bold and to rely more on defensive tactics. Attrition and his inability to replace his losses had deprived Lee of his power to make sustained attacks. His brilliant defensive campaign in 1864 made the Federals pay in manpower as they had never paid before, but Lee turned to defensive warfare too late and with too few men. Unlike the Federals, he had already exhausted his manpower reserves.

Renewed Union Confidence. The fall of Vicksburg and the defeat of Lee at Gettysburg restored confidence in the North. The Union navy had closed all the important Confederate Atlantic ports except Charleston, South Carolina, and Wilmington, North Carolina, and these were blockaded by Federal warships. A Union amphibious expedition threatened Charleston. The South—cut in half—was short of men, equipment, and food. Moreover, Confederate forces in Tennessee were about to be pushed back into Georgia.

Chickamauga. No major action took place in Tennessee from January, when Bragg retreated after Murfreesboro, until Rosecrans advanced toward Chattanooga in June 1863. Bragg, outflanked by the Federals, evacuated Chattanooga and twice failed in attempts to attack Rosecrans's divided army. President Davis, deciding that additional troops would help, sent Longstreet's Corps from Lee's Army of Northern Virginia to reinforce Bragg. On September 19, Bragg attacked the Federals in northern Georgia near Chickamauga Creek. The next day the Confederates discovered a gap in the Union line, rushed through it, and the Federal position soon collapsed. Rosecrans

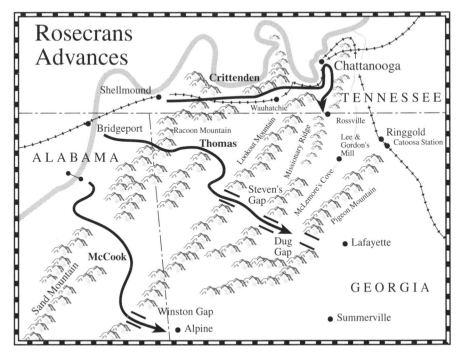

Rosecrans
Advances

Chattanooga

Crittenden

Shellmound

TENNESSEE

Wauhatchie

Rossville

Bridgeport

Racoon Mountain

Thomas

Lee & Gordon's Mill

Ringgold

Catoosa Station

ALABAMA

Lookout Mountain

Missionary Ridge

Steven's Gap

McLemore's Cove

Pigeon Mountain

Dug Gap

Lafayette

McCook

Sand Mountain

GEORGIA

Winston Gap

Alpine

Summerville

and most of his army retreated into Chattanooga. Only one corps, under Gen. George Thomas ("The Rock of Chickamauga"), held on until night. At Chickamauga, one of the few battles in which the Confederates outnumbered the Federals, Bragg lost 17,000 of 66,000 men and Rosecrans lost 11,000 of 58,000 men.

Missionary Ridge. After Chickamauga, the Confederates took positions on the heights south of Chattanooga. But their attempt to starve the Federals into surrendering—as the Confederates had been forced to do at Vicksburg—failed. Bragg, in disagreement with some of his generals, weakened his siege by allowing Longstreet to take part of the army on an unsuccessful and reckless effort to capture Knoxville, Tennessee. Grant, now Union commander in the West, replaced Rosecrans with Thomas, who opened a safe supply line into the town to feed the hungry Federals. Grant arrived with reinforcements, including Hooker's Corps from the East, which, on November 24, he sent against the foggy face of Lookout Mountain, one of the two big heights commanding Chattanooga. Hooker drove the Confederates off the mountain, and the next day Grant attacked the second key height, Missionary Ridge. When his assault on Bragg's right flank went awry, Grant ordered Thomas to reconnoiter the trenches at the foot of the ridge. On November 25, Thomas's men advanced on the trenches and then, without orders, rushed up and cleared the Confederates from Missionary Ridge. Badly defeated, the Confederates retreated into Georgia. As for casualties in these actions around Chattanooga, the Federals lost only 6,000 of 63,000 effectives, and the Confederates 7,000 of 44,000.

An Excellent Year for the North. The news of Grant's victory at Missionary Ridge reached the North on Thanksgiving Day. The year had begun glumly, but Northerners were now hopeful after their tremendous victories at Vicksburg, Gettysburg, and Missionary Ridge. Not only was the entire Mississippi Valley under Federal control, but Union armies had opened a gateway into the central Confederacy. Many Northerners now believed that the power of the Confederacy had been broken. "The crisis," said Lincoln, "which threatens to divide the friends of the Union is past." Events seemed to justify such optimism, yet hard fighting remained.

Chapter Eleven

TO THE END

Grant Becomes Commanding General. In February 1864, Congress revived the military rank of lieutenant general—a title held hitherto only by George Washington and Winfield Scott—and authorized the President to promote to that rank the major general who was most distinguished for courage, skill, and ability. Lincoln called Grant to the capital and named him commanding general. But Grant refused to sit behind a desk in Washington and wanted to stay in the field. Having turned over command of the western army to his friend Gen. William T. Sherman, Grant decided to establish his headquarters with General Meade's army.

Grant's Strategy. Grant planned to apply pressure everywhere on the Confederacy, exchange no prisoners, and use the North's manpower and resources to overwhelm the South and wear it down. Meade—directed by Grant—would focus on Lee's army in Virginia, and Sherman would concentrate on Bragg's old army, now commanded by Joseph E. Johnston, in Georgia. Sherman and Meade were to keep fighting continuously regardless of weather or season. Theirs was to be a concentric movement designed to press the life out of the Confederacy. Grant intended to use all of the Union armies—not just Sherman's and Meade's. He wanted to send one commanded by Gen. Nathaniel P. Banks to take Mobile, but Lincoln prevented that by granting Banks's

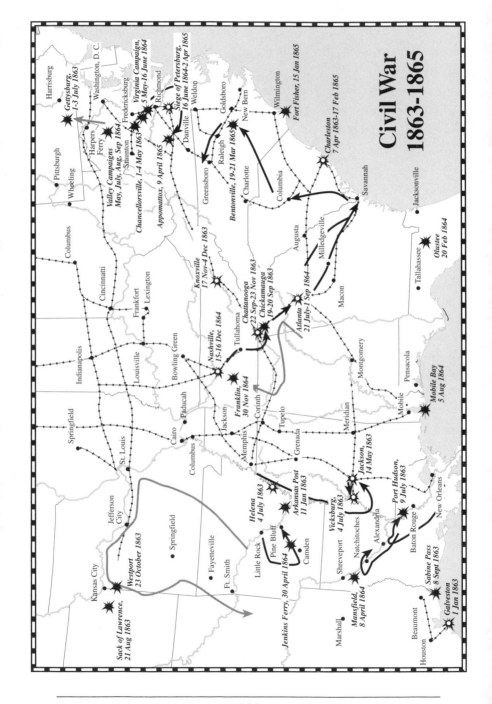

Civil War 1863-1865

request to move up the Red River against Shreveport, the temporary capital of Louisiana and a major supply depot as well as the gateway to Texas.

The Red River Campaign. The river campaign began in March 1864. Gunboats transported Federal troops up the Red River toward Shreveport where General Banks expected to join Gen. Frederick Steele and 15,000 men marching down from Little Rock, Arkansas. On May 8, Confederate Gen. Richard Taylor, son of the old Mexican War general, defeated Banks at Mansfield, south of Shreveport. The following day the Federals made a stand at Pleasant Hill before continuing their withdrawal. The gunboats and the army, harassed by Taylor's men, retreated down the river. Low water at Alexandria held up the gunboats, but by the end of May, the Union vessels and soldiers were safe and the Red River Campaign was over. It had accomplished nothing other than to antagonize most of the planters along the river, who had burned their cotton rather than let the Federals confiscate it.

The Wilderness. On May 4, in Virginia, Meade's army—119,000 strong—crossed the Rapidan River west of Chancellorsville. Ten months of carnage followed. The first action occurred in the heavily wooded terrain near Chancellorsville known as the Wilderness, where Lee waited with 64,000 men. On May 6, after a day of blind fighting, Longstreet advanced and wrecked a Federal attack. By May 7, Lee had managed to turn both Federal flanks, and Grant broke off the action. But instead of retreating, he moved around Lee's right toward Richmond. The Wilderness was a tactical victory for Lee—he lost only 8,000 to Grant's 15,000—but Grant seemed determined to press on toward Richmond, giving the weakened Confederates no time to recover.

Spotsylvania. Lee won the race to the next strong point—at Spotsylvania Court House—and had entrenched his army by

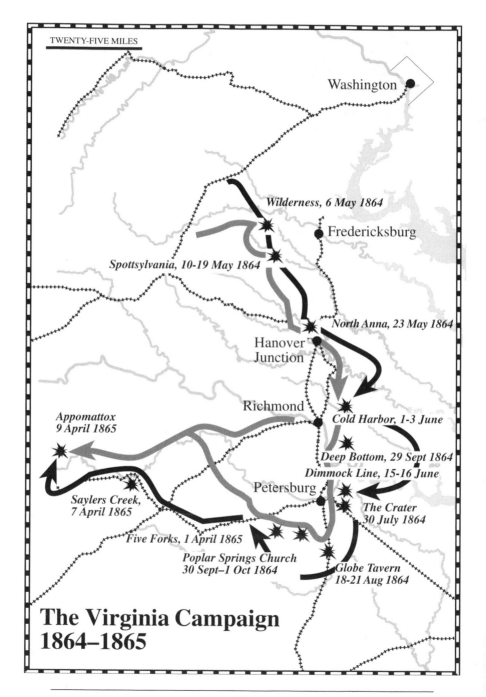

TWENTY-FIVE MILES

Washington

Wilderness, 6 May 1864

Fredericksburg

Spottsylvania, 10-19 May 1864

North Anna, 23 May 1864

Hanover Junction

Richmond

Appomattox
9 April 1865

Cold Harbor, 1-3 June

Deep Bottom, 29 Sept 1864

Dimmock Line, 15-16 June

Petersburg

Saylers Creek,
7 April 1865

The Crater
30 July 1864

Five Forks, 1 April 1865

Poplar Springs Church
30 Sept–1 Oct 1864

Globe Tavern
18-21 Aug 1864

The Virginia Campaign
1864–1865

the time Grant attacked on May 9. For more than a week, Federals struck at the Confederate defense line, but finally, unable to overwhelm Lee, Grant disengaged his army and once again moved around Lee's right toward Richmond. Of the approximately 90,000 Federals engaged, Grant lost 17,000; of the approximately 50,000 Confederates, Lee lost 9,000. Although the Confederates had inflicted heavier losses on the Federals, Grant retained the initiative.

Cold Harbor. Each Federal movement brought Grant closer to Richmond. On May 23 the Federals encountered Lee's entrenched army along the North Anna River. After two days of skirmishing followed by a day of hard fighting, Grant broke off his attack and marched southward toward Mechanicsville. There Grant found Lee's main line too strong and moved south a fourth time to discover the wily Lee dug in again at Cold Harbor. After inadequate reconnaissance, Grant sent three Union corps against Lee's strong fieldworks. The main attack failed, although smaller actions continued from June 1 to 12. Cold Harbor was a bloody defeat for Grant. He lost 7,000 of his 108,000 men; Lee lost 1,500 of his 59,000.

Petersburg. On June 12, Grant moved his army south of the James River and joined Gen. Benjamin Butler's army on the outskirts of Petersburg, just south of Richmond. This maneuver fooled Lee, but the uncoordinated Federal assaults failed to drive the outnumbered Confederates from Petersburg. By June 22, Lee had arrived with the rest of his army. Tedious trench warfare followed, foreshadowing the terrible carnage on the western front in World War I. On July 30, Federal miners set off a great explosive charge under the Confederate works. As Union troops swarmed into the crater, the Confederates counterattacked and in the colossal confusion killed 4,000 Federals. For the remainder of the year Grant extended his entrenchments southward and westward trying to cut Lee's supply lines. To meet this threat, Lee had to stretch his defense ever thinner. By winter there was only one railroad open to Petersburg.

Elsewhere in the East. Meanwhile, small armies fought elsewhere in the East. Federal Gen. David Hunter marched from the Shenandoah Valley toward Richmond only to be defeated and forced back into West Virginia by Confederate Gen. Jubal Early, who then rampaged down the valley into Maryland. Early reached the defenses of Washington, but his forces were too weak to attack the capital. Grant sent Gen. Philip Sheridan and a new army after Early. At Winchester, Virginia, on September 19, Sheridan lost 5,000 of his 35,000 men defeating Early's 12,000 Confederates, who suffered 3,500 casualties. Sheridan's waves of horsemen and infantry were too much for Early's small army.

Battles for Atlanta. In the western theater, Sherman started south from Chattanooga toward Atlanta in May 1864. Using his army of 100,000 men in flanking movements, Sherman pushed Johnston's 49,000 men back across northern Georgia. The Union army was checked when it attacked Johnston's strong fieldworks at Kennesaw Mountain, and Sherman quickly returned to his more successful and less costly flanking movements. When the Confederates eventually fell back to the outskirts of Atlanta, President Davis replaced Johnston with Gen. John Bell Hood. Sherman guessed correctly that Hood would attack and prepared his army accordingly. In nine days Sherman defeated Hood three times—at Peachtree Creek, in the Battle of Atlanta itself, and at Ezra Church. Late in August, Sherman cut Atlanta's supply lines, forcing Hood to get out or starve. Hood abandoned the town, which Sherman occupied on September 2. The fall of Atlanta was a major loss for the Confederates. Johnston's retreat through north Georgia in May

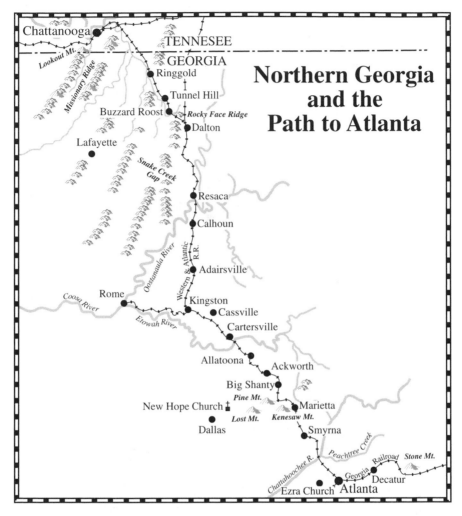

Northern Georgia and the Path to Atlanta

and June cost the Federals 3,000 more men than Johnston lost, whereas Hood's attacks on Union forces around Atlanta from late July to early September cost the Confederates 12,500 more men than Sherman lost.

Presidential Election. Lincoln believed that the fall of Atlanta was responsible for his reelection. Renominated by the Republican or National Union Convention in June, with Andrew

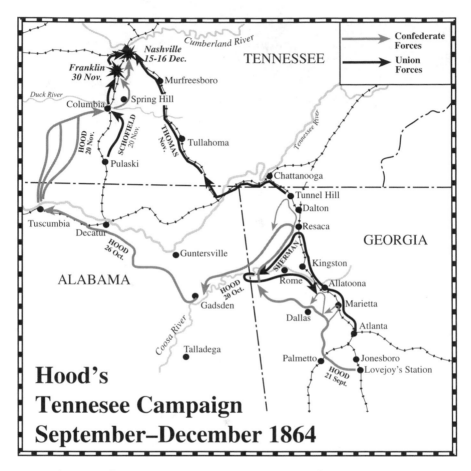

| Confederate Forces |
| Union Forces |

Hood's Tennesee Campaign September–December 1864

Johnson of Tennessee, a War Democrat, as his running mate, Lincoln feared that he would be defeated. The Democrats nominated Gen. George B. McClellan for President and George H. Pendleton of Ohio for Vice President. Their platform, influenced strongly by anti-Lincoln men, designated "Copperheads" by their Republican enemies, called for immediately ending the war and restoring peace. Pacifism and defeatism throughout the North in midsummer dimmed the prospects of Lincoln's reelection. Some Radical Republicans even proposed replacing Lincoln with another nominee, but the capture of Atlanta changed the election outlook and induced the Radicals to unite behind Lincoln, who won by 212 to 21 electoral votes, but received a popular majority of only 400,000 out of 4,000,000 votes.

Franklin. After abandoning Atlanta, Hood moved north and west into Tennessee. He hoped to achieve victories that would offset not only his loss of Atlanta but Union Commander David Farragut's victory in Mobile Bay, which closed the Confederacy's last big seaport on the Gulf. Hood had fantastic plans: defeat the Federals, recruit new soldiers in Tennessee, and then move eastward to reinforce Lee. Sherman's counterplans were more realistic. Leaving behind Thomas and enough troops to contain Hood, Sherman moved from Atlanta southeastward across Georgia with 62,000 men toward Savannah on his "March to the Sea." Thomas rushed to fortify Nashville and sent Gen. John Schofield to watch Hood's movements. Schofield, after escaping from a fight at Columbia and a trap at Spring Hill, withdrew northward to Franklin, Tennessee, where his 28,000 troops hastily dug fieldworks. Hood followed and sent his 23,000 Confederates in a grand charge across a half mile of open ground against the Federal works. Confederate losses were over 6,000, including six generals killed, five wounded, and one captured. Federal losses were a little over 1,000. Franklin was a disaster for the Confederacy.

Nashville. After Franklin, Hood continued on to Nashville and placed his demoralized men on hills outside the town. In two days of fighting on December 15-16, Thomas's 50,000 men crushed Hood's weak line. After losing 6,000 men—twice as many as the Federals—Hood retreated. Nashville was his last battle. As the wreckage of the Confederate army limped southward, the soliders sang: "The Gallant Hood of Texas Played Hell in Tennessee."

Sherman's March. While Hood was destroying his army in Tennessee, Sherman was marching through Georgia and the

Carolinas, carrying out as he went a policy of total war. After burning Atlanta, he moved toward Savannah, methodically destroying anything that might be useful to the Confederacy. Promising Georgia's governor that he would "devastate the State in its whole length and breadth," Sherman informed Grant, "Until we can repopulate Georgia, it is useless for us to occupy it; but [its] . . . utter destruction . . . will cripple their military resources. I can make . . . Georgia howl." Indeed, he did. Sherman's 60,000 men, marching along four parallel roads, laid waste a strip of country sixty miles wide and three hundred miles long. Small Confederate units sniped at Sherman's men, but no major army opposed the Federals. On December 22, Sherman captured Savannah and presented it to Lincoln as a Christmas present. Estimating that his troops had inflicted $100,000,000 worth of damage on Georgia, Sherman admitted that eighty percent of this was "simple waste and destruction." Union troops remained in Savannah about a month and then, with his army stronger than it was when he left Atlanta, Sherman moved northward through South Carolina and into North Carolina. Joseph E. Johnston, who had scrapped together about 15,000 Confederates, attacked one wing of Sherman's army at Bentonville, North Carolina, on March 19-20, 1865. Johnston's men held their own until the remainder of Sherman's army forced them to withdraw. Sherman seized a railroad at Goldsboro and bivouacked to await word from Grant.

Breaking the Petersburg Line. Lee's army still held the Petersburg trenches, but the men had suffered through the long winter months. Food supplies shrank, and bitterly cold weather sickened hungry men dressed in rags and without overcoats or tents. Disease plagued the Confederates and their numbers dwindled to 28,000 men as Grant continued a slow extension of the Union lines. Lee had no choice but to lengthen his own lines. On March 25, 1865, he lost 5,000 men in a desperate attempt to break Grant's hold at the north end of the siege line. Having secured his right, Grant sent Sheridan on April 1 to the far left to gain control of Lee's only remaining supply line—the South Side Railroad. The Confederates resisted, but Sheridan's numbers overwhelmed them. Grant then attacked all along the Petersburg line, and Lee's thin defenses collapsed. Lee managed to hold on long enough for the Confederate government to abandon Richmond, but he failed in his effort to join Johnston's army. On April 9, after losing a third of his men in a hard fight at Sayler's Creek, Lee surrendered his encircled army of 13,000 men to Grant at Appomattox Courthouse.

The Confederacy Collapses. President Davis and his cabinet fled Richmond hoping to continue the struggle elsewhere. The surrender, first of Lee to Grant and then of Johnston to Sherman near Durham, North Carolina, on April 26, caused the government to disband. Davis still hoped to reach some unsurrendered army that would fight on, but on May 10 Union forces captured him in Georgia. Sent to Fort Monroe, Virginia, he remained a prisoner until 1867, when he was finally released on bail. On May 4, Gen. Richard Taylor surrendered his army at Citronelle, Alabama, and on May 26, Gen. Edmund Kirby Smith surrendered the Confederacy's last major army at New Orleans. The war was over.

Lincoln's Assassination. On April 14, 1865, President Lincoln, after working on plans for the restoration of peace and conciliation, was shot by actor John Wilkes Booth while attending a Washington theater. Carried unconscious to a house across the street, Lincoln died there the next morning.

The Cost. The Civil War was the bloodiest war in American history. Casualties totaled nearly forty percent of the combined Union and Confederate armies. Authorities disagree on the exact figures, but the Federals suffered more than 600,000 casualties (over half killed) and the Confederates sustained about 400,000 casualties (more than a quarter of a million killed). Of the million men who fought for the Confederacy, more than a fourth died of wounds or disease. If, in relation to the southern white population, the North had suffered commensurately it would have lost more than 1,000,000 men instead of 360,000. With the same comparison, the American colonies in revolt against England would have lost 94,000 men instead of 12,000, and the United States in World War II would have lost well over 6,000,000 men instead of somewhat more than 300,000. "The Confederacy," a scholar noted, "rendered the heaviest sacrifices in lives . . . ever made by Americans."

The Legacy. The Civil War had disrupted a way of life and changed the course of American history as significantly as the French Revolution and the Russian Revolution changed French and Russian history. The War for Southern Independence destroyed the South's America as well as the America of the Founding Fathers. The strong national state that emerged from the war outlawed secession and slavery, but it also replaced the old federal republic that had protected a citizen's liberties from encroachment. The postwar national government enjoyed extraordinary powers, including the authority to tax people directly and to put them in jail if they refused to pay, to draft men into the army, to create a national currency and a national bank system, to expand the jurisdiction of federal courts, and to establish the first national agency for social welfare—the Freedmen's Bureau. All but one of the first twelve amendments to the Constitution had limited the powers of the federal government, but the next six, starting in 1865 with the Thirteenth Amendment abolishing slavery, increased federal powers at the expense of the states. The Fourteenth and Fifteenth Amendments, which placed citizenship and voting protection squarely in federal hands for the first time, at least held promises for black Southerners about equality in society. But even with those amendments in place, the federal government eventually failed to back them in ways that would ensure equality to black Americans.

The strengthening of the national government during and after the war accompanied a shift of political power from the South to the North. Before the sectional conflict—for the first seventy-two years of the republic—Southerners had been President of the United States two-thirds of the time. In the national Congress, during the same period, twenty-four of the Senate's presidents pro tem and twenty-three of the House's thirty-six speakers had been Southerners. A majority of Southerners had always dominated the antebellum Supreme Court. But after the Civil War a hundred years passed before a resident of an ex-Confederate state was elected president. For fifty years none of the presidents pro tem of the Senate or speakers of the House came from the South, and during that same half-century only five of the twenty-six appointees to the Supreme Court were Southerners.

White Southerners paid a high price for their attempt to gain independence. More than a quarter of a million of them, a whole generation, died in the struggle, and for more than a century, the war's legacy of mistrust and bitterness prevented Southerners from sharing equally, as they had earlier, in governing and shaping the country. Perhaps most devastating of all, following the war, the South was reduced to a colonial status for decades to come.

Index

For more information about the people and places mentioned in *The Civil War*, check out the Civil War Campaign and Commanders Series by the McWhiney Foundation Press. Titles include...

Battle in the Wilderness: Grant Meets Lee by Grady McWhiney ❖ Death in September: The Antietam Campaign by Perry D. Jamieson ❖ Texans in the Confederate Cavalry by Anne J. Bailey ❖ Sam Bell Maxey and the Confederate Indians by John C. Waugh ❖ The Saltville Massacre by Thomas D. Mays ❖ General James Longstreet in the West: A Monumental Failure by Judith Lee Hallock ❖ The Battle of the Crater by Jeff Kinard ❖ Cottonclads! The Battle of Galveston and the Defense of the Texas Coast by Donald S. Frazier ❖ A Deep, Steady Thunder: The Battle of Chickamauga by Steven E. Woodworth ❖ The Texas Overland Expedition by Richard Lowe ❖ Raphael Semmes and the Alabama by Spencer C. Tucker ❖ War in the West: Pea Ridge and Prairie Grove by William L. Shea ❖ Iron and Heavy Guns: Duel Between the Monitor and Merrimac by Gene A. Smith ❖ The Emergence of Total War by Daniel E. Sutherland ❖ John Bell Hood and the Struggle for Atlanta by David Coffey ❖ The Most Promising Young Man of the South: James Johnston Pettigrew and His Men at Gettysburg by Clyde N. Wilson ❖ Vicksburg: Fall of the Confederate Gibraltar by Terrence J. Winschel ❖ This Grand Spectacle: The Battle of Chattanooga by Steven E. Woodworth ❖ Rutherford B. Hayes: "One of the Good Colonels" by Ari Hoogenboom ❖ Jefferson Davis's Greatest General: Albert Sidney Johnston by Charles P. Roland ❖ Unconditional Surrender: The Capture of Forts Henry and Donelson by Spencer C. Tucker ❖ Last Stand at Mobile by John C. Waugh ❖ George Gordon Meade and the War in the East by Ethan S. Rafuse ❖ Winfield Scott Hancock: Gettysburg Hero by Perry D. Jamieson ❖ The Last Stronghold: The Campaign for Fort Fisher by Richard B. McCaslin ❖ Sherman's March to the Sea by John Marszalek

These books available at booksellers or through Texas A&M University Press Consortium at 1-800-826-8911 or on-line at www.tamu.edu/upress

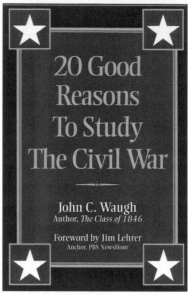